I0797372

Joy Chose You

PRAISE FOR DONNA ASHWORTH

"Donna Ashworth has a way of formulating words that melts me... I feel as if the universe has sent me her book to tell me I'm on the right course."
Davina McCall

"Powerful and comforting ... Donna's words could change your life."
Dawn French

"Absolutely beautiful... Whenever I'm feeling lost, I reach for Donna Ashworth's words and feel found."
Bryony Gordon

"Some people have the Bible by their bed. Others a self-help manual. I have Donna Ashworth."
Susannah Constantine

"If there is a god, Donna is doing her or his work."
Robbie Williams

"So inspiring, so heartfelt... the way Donna writes is beyond beautiful."
Lisa Snowdon

"Soul-nurturing permission to relax, connect and be kinder to ourselves."
Fearne Cotton

"A little corner of calm within life's storm - wonderful."
Cat Deeley

"Donna's words are never just words, they are teachings. Provoking and inspiring, comforting and loving, I couldn't live without them."
Kellie Bright

"Donna's much-needed words will no doubt empower and lift our young people today."
Lisa Faulkner

"Like a warm hug. Donna's words are comfort for the soul."
Tamzin Outhwaite

"Donna has a rare gift of being able to put into words how we all feel. Her writing is like a hug from a wise friend."
Samia Longchambon

"Donna is a true wordsmith. Her writings never fail to move me."
Nadia Sawalha

"Brilliantly reflective, awakening and full of comfort."
Giovanna Fletcher

DONNA
ASHWORTH

Joy Chose You

HAY HOUSE LLC
Carlsbad, California • New York City
London • Sydney • New Delhi

To my darling boys:
you brought with you
a depth of joy
I barely knew.

Published in the United States by: Hay House LLC, www.hayhouse.com®
P.O. Box 5100, Carlsbad, CA, 92018-5100

Design and Illustration by: Emma Wells for Studio Nic+Lou
Photo of Donna Ashworth: © Donna Ashworth

First published in the UK in 2025 by Blink, an imprint of Bonnier Books UK, 5th Floor, HYLO, 105 Bunhill Row, London, EC1Y 8LZ.
ISBN: 978-1-7853-0845-1

Cataloging-in-Publication Data is on file at the Library of Congress

Hardcover ISBN: 979-8-3186-0164-4
E-book ISBN: 979-8-3186-0165-1
Audiobook ISBN: 979-8-3186-0166-8

10 9 8 7 6 5 4 3 2 1

1st US edition, November 2025

Printed in the United States of America

This product uses responsibly sourced papers, including recycled materials and materials from other controlled sources.

The authorized representative in the EU for product safety and compliance is Penguin Random House Ireland, Morrison Chambers, 32 Nassau Street, Dublin D02 YH68, Ireland. https://eu-contact.penguin.ie

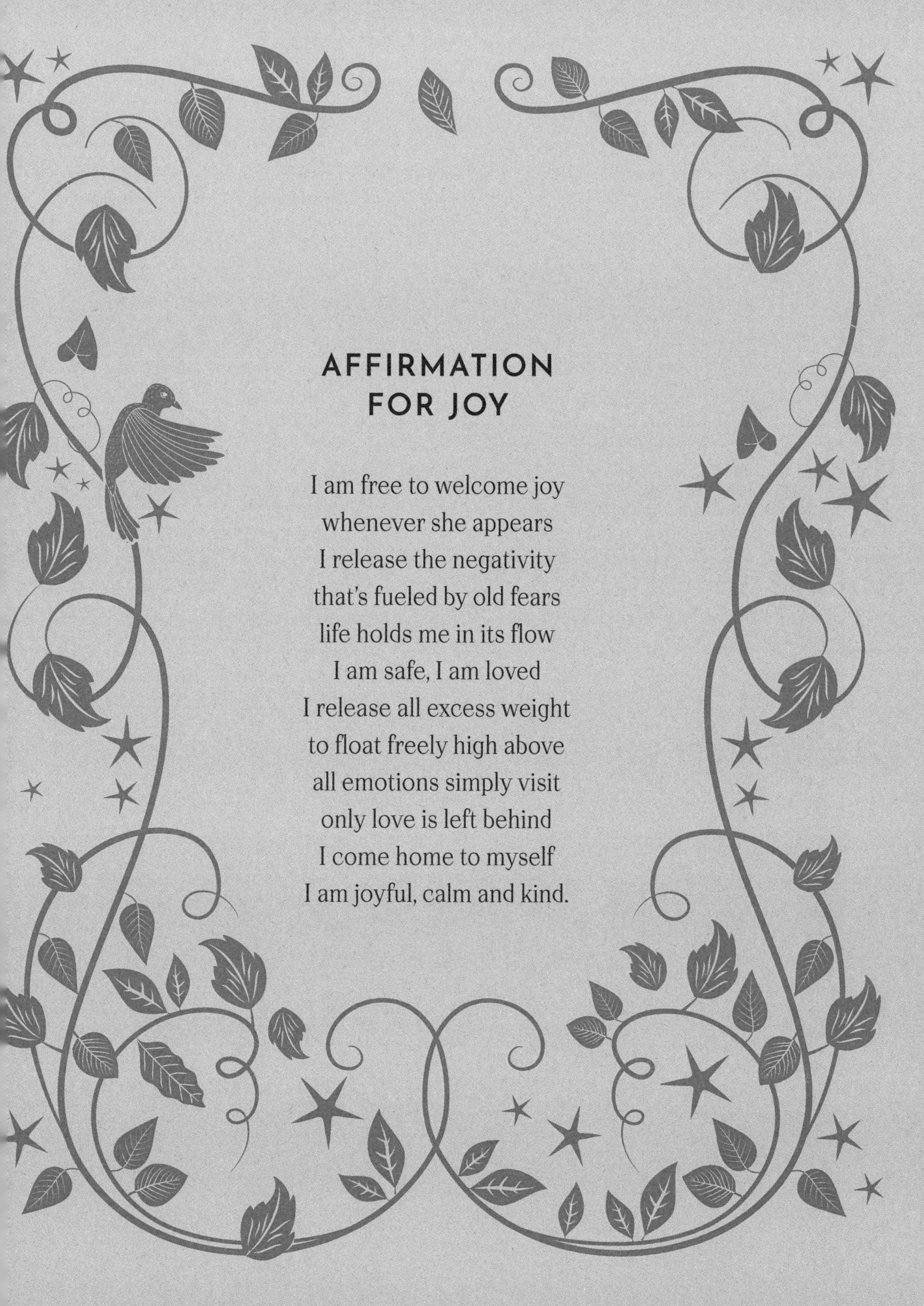

AFFIRMATION FOR JOY

I am free to welcome joy
whenever she appears
I release the negativity
that's fueled by old fears
life holds me in its flow
I am safe, I am loved
I release all excess weight
to float freely high above
all emotions simply visit
only love is left behind
I come home to myself
I am joyful, calm and kind.

CONTENTS

WELCOME

Welcome to this collection of all my favorites, and yours, from the past few years. One of the things I am asked most often is which book can certain poems be found in. So, from a practical point of view, this anthology made sense. A place to gather all the most-loved (and most-used) passages in one beautiful place, for your gifting and reading pleasure.

From a heart-led point of view, this book is an oasis. I hope you will pick her up whenever life is beating you down and I hope that in this doing, magic will be unleashed. Because the book knows. Try a random page every day and see what happens. The message may be one that your brain very much needs, or perhaps it will be for your soul, your inner child, your pain, your courageous gut. Or for someone you love dearly and for whom you very much wish to find the right words.

Whatever it brings, I promise you it will be uplifting. For the title of this book reminds us that even in the hardest of climbs, the darkest of times, joy can find us. And to host joy well is not to become a constant source of positivity, but rather to be accepting that life is all things. To welcome in all the emotions, sit with them for a heartbeat or two before allowing them to move on as they must.

As they say: this too shall pass...

Yet this means that the good times will also pass. And that's okay. Because they all come back. No need to squeeze joy tight when she appears and keep grasp of her. She will not stay. But if you are a gracious host, she will return. In the same way sadness will pay you a visit now and then too. Oftentimes we panic, block the doorway, when we should really just let her in for tea. She means no harm; she is just heartache and pain. A side product of this life and its many losses. A side product of the privilege of love.

Nothing is linear in this life, you see; everything loops. And we are simply here to flow with and make the most of each sunrise we are gifted. Seizing the flashes of brilliance when they spark and hunkering down with love through the storms that shake our foundations.

We need one another on this journey. And this book was made to be gifted to others, and to yourself, too. For without a decent friendship with yourself, no other relationship can truly flourish.

Enjoy this book; I infused her with energy, understanding, compassion and hope. She is love. And you deserve that. It is an honor to be in your hands right now.

Hands on your beating heart, breathe deeply into your miraculous life-givers...and on we go.

You

deserve

that

joy

right

now

NOW

If you can decide to find joy
in whatever is around you
right now
you are entering a whole new realm
of peace
where the wars and storms can rage
but you will still be you
finding happiness and contentment
in the everyday moments
allowing your heart to break
as it must

you deserve that joy right now
not in a year
not when you are more
not when *everything falls into place*

now.

BECOMING

You are always becoming
the person you were born to be
before the world began to mold you
to its pattern
and not your own

you are always becoming

she who learned to hide
and shape-shift
to suit the crowd
the mood, the room

you are always becoming
and every time you release
a little more of her
to the world
I like to think Mother Nature
breathes out
exhales
a little more deeply...

here she is...

keep becoming
keep becoming.

"We must
let them
interchange
like the
sun and
the moon"

HAPPY

They say happiness is a choice, but I think it's like day and night. We cannot be happy all of the time, nor can we be continuously sad. We must let them interchange, like the sun and the moon. That's the cycle, you see. And yet, they can exist together sometimes too, a little strangely, a little awkwardly perhaps. Reminding us life isn't black and white, that emotions are every color. And nothing is constant. They say happiness is a choice, but I think it's peace that we can choose, peace in the acceptance that life is everything. And that's okay. A baseline of peace invites happiness to stay a little longer and lets sadness come and go, as it must. As it all must.

Beautiful

moments

are

everywhere

waiting

to be seen

MAGIC

You must believe in the magic. Even on the dreariest of days, when light is scarce, you must leave space in your heart for the good stuff to thrive. Let it in. Look for it. Beautiful moments are everywhere, waiting to be seen. And each time you see one amongst the mire, you're reminding every cell in your body that life is so much more than days in a week and chores on a list. It is a patchwork kaleidoscope of absolutely everything. And you are a fascinating, complicated part of that art.

DON'T MISS YOUR OWN PARTY

When you prepare for days to ensure a gathering
is the most perfect it can possibly be

but you miss the whole thing
because you are so very busy
doing and not *being*

don't let that be the metaphor for your life

don't let the moment you finally relax
be a moment too far

I guess what I am trying to say is
don't miss your own party
because you wanted everyone else
to have the best time

now is the time to sit down
take a beat and chat with a friend
or loved one
now is the time to eat
break bread and be merry
now is the time to be fully here
fully present, enjoying, experiencing
living

not after
not when everything is perfect

the dishes can wait
this is your party
your life
you're invited too.

"Joy is
supposed
to slip
through
the cracks"

JOY CHOSE YOU

Joy does not arrive with a fanfare
on a red carpet strewn
with the flowers of a perfect life

joy sneaks in
as you pour a cup of coffee
watching the sunlight
hit your favorite tree
just right

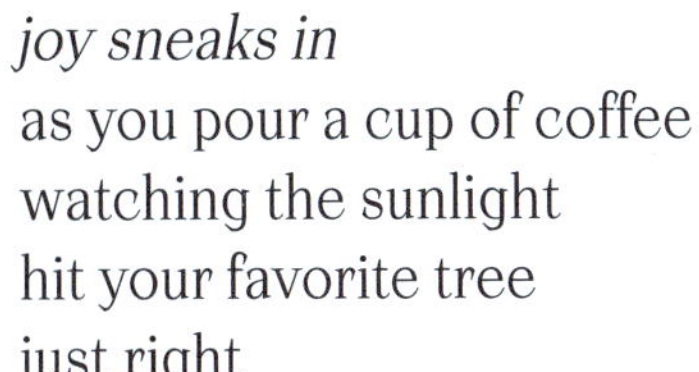

and you usher joy away
because you are not ready for her
your house is not as it should be
for such a distinguished guest

but joy, you see
cares nothing for your messy home
or your bank balance
or your waistline

joy is *supposed* to slip through
the cracks of your imperfect life
that's how joy *works*

you cannot truly invite her
you can only be ready
when she appears
and hug her with meaning
because in this very moment
joy chose you.

KNOW YOURSELF

Know yourself, they say
and don't be led astray
but how can I know who I am
when I'm different every day?

some days I'm the smart one
with the answers people need
and some days I'm the strong one
standing up to take the lead.

on other days I'm sure
that if the wind blew me too hard
I would shatter like a glass
into a million tiny shards

and on those days I cower
and I hide out from the world
waiting on my inner child
to blossom and unfurl

and each day I'm surprised
by the newness that I see
the things I'm finding out
the complexity of me

so how to know yourself
when you're all things rolled in one?
you simply must decide
to love whatever you become.

UNSTOPPABLE

Unstoppable, they called her
but I saw her stop
I saw her stop
many, many times

sometimes
I thought she had stopped
for good

but no
she always found a way
to resurrect

to rise again

not the same
never the same

each time a little more determined
and a little less vulnerable

unstoppable, they said
but I think
it was in the stopping

that she found
her power.

If only
we could
realize
resting
is very
much *doing*

REST

If only we could see the power in rest. If only we could attach to it the worth it so deserves. If only we could open our minds to the idea that everything in nature has its time to rise and its time to descend. That each of these acts is as important as the other. And that is exactly as it must be. If only the ability to allow our bodies space to heal was awarded the same badge of honor given to busyness and stress in this life. If only we could realize, resting is very much *doing*.

SITTING WITH JOY

I sat with joy and asked her
how she keeps her candor up
how she floats above the misery
and from where her cup's filled up

does she not see the suffering
can she not hear those cries
do angels block her ears
as she floats through cloud-free
skies

what of all the misery
the love that's torn apart
to know this world is hard, yet
the softest thing's the heart

and joy, she sweetly listened
soft humor round her eyes
she reached across the table
speaking words that tell no lies

this life is not for fear, love
let steel give way to flow
resist the urge to hoard
let all things come and go

when grief is on your doorstep
let her in and bend the knee
face the pain, from love it came
acceptance sets you free

I also bow to darkness
and let it stroke my soul
knowing that it cannot break
for light will keep me whole

and when that light blinds in
and the chaos filters out
I'm ready then, with open arms
no place in me for doubt

to work, I set my focus
to spread more love than hate
from door to door I fly
the cracks become my gate

so yes, I hear the cries too
and yes, they hurt my core
but tears will not dry tears, love
only hope can lift and soar

so hope I bring and love I sing
to heal, day in day out
and of my cup? this fills it up
of this there is no doubt.

"Give in
to the
slumber
you
crave"

BEFORE YOU SLEEP

Leave guilt on the floor
by your slippers and robe
your worries may nestle there too
let shame and embarrassment
slip through the door
there's no place for such things here with you

let memories of laughter
words aimed to warm
fill up any space in your head
remember the smiles
of the people you love
let those treasures come with you to bed

you did all you could
with the day that you had
you led with that heart full of love
you toil and you care
and that's *always* enough
so release that dark load to above

now rest, close your eyes
let your fears melt away
give in to the slumber you crave
you are giving your all
to this cycle of life
welcome dreams and await a new day.

SAY IT

Never be afraid
to let someone know
if they brightened the room
they just walked into

or if something they said
inspired you to change

never be embarrassed
to share a compliment with a stranger
and don't ever fall into the trap of believing
that the people you love *know* that

say it
always say it

your words may land a little awkwardly at first
but in the still of the night
those seeds will plant themselves
into someone's mental garden
and start to germinate
gather strength and bloom

there is nothing better you can do with your words
than plant a precious seed

sow seeds wherever you go
cast your love and watch it grow.

“The
quickest
route back
to self
to inner
peace is
bare feet
on grass”

YOU ARE NATURE

There is a reason why walking amongst nature is most people's best advice when depression strikes. Because walking in nature is a return to *home*. You are not a lover of nature or in need of some nature; you *are* nature. You are as much nature as the trees in your garden and the bees on your picnic. You were designed to live your days out in the wild with your fellow creatures and plants, but progress, *humanity*, had different plans for us all. And so we exist day-to-day, in our homes, but never *home*. The quickest route back to self, to inner peace, is bare feet on grass, arms around trees, head in the clouds and heart in a forest. Put your weary body in water, whenever you can. Smell every flower you see and crumble dirt between your tired-of-typing fingers. You *are* nature, so go home once in a while. It will bring you so much you didn't even know you were missing.

SHE GATHERED

She gathered things along the way to pass on
but not beautiful clothes or jewels

she gathered starlight when she couldn't sleep
and sprinkled it on her stories
so that the children of her children
would listen in wonder and remember with delight

she gathered lessons learned at rock bottom
and shared them with strangers and friends alike
to save them the need to sink so far themselves

she gathered precious, life-giving laughter
and regaled the world with the humorous reminiscing
of her follies, her foibles and her mishaps

she gathered things
that may not have caught anyone's eye in auction
but when examined closely
became true treasure maps
to this life's gold mines.

I MISSED YOU TODAY

I missed you today but that's nothing new
I missed you a million times yesterday too
I picked up my phone to tell you the news
then realized, again, I can't text it to you

I saw your bright smile, at least twenty times
and then I remember, it's all in my mind
I drive without presence, the world feels surreal
and on comes your song and this doesn't seem real

I missed you today but I miss you a lot
it's helpful to miss you, it's all that I've got
I wish I could pull you down here for a while
I'm frightened to lose the shape of your smile

I miss you today and I'll miss you tomorrow
there seems to be no coming end to this sorrow
I try to go on as I know that you care
I know that you're willing me on from up there

I miss you today but I'm trying to find
a way to move on but not leave you behind
a way to forge on with the love that we had
a way to recall you and simply feel... glad.

"You'll look at
the mountain
ahead of you
and realize
you've done
it before"

MOUNTAINS

Oh but you must look behind you sometimes or you may not recall the mountains. The ones you thought you'd die on. The ones you scaled and survived with such bravery and passion. And then you'll look at the mountain ahead of you and realize you've done it before. You've done much harder before, in fact. And you'll do it *again.* Oh but you must look behind you sometimes, my love, even if just to see how very much you are.

THIS IS NO WAITING ROOM

What if you didn't wake up tomorrow
and your soul is watching down
thinking of all the things you didn't get to do yet
because you were too scared
or too shy
or too worried about money

and all the things you told yourself
you weren't good enough for
swam in front of your eyes
fighting for a place in the line
beside the words you didn't say
and the joy you forgot to have

my friend, there is absolutely no room
for anything in your day
other than *acceptance*
you will never have enough money, or time
and you will certainly never have that perfect body
the world told you to want to be happy

and before you say it's too late
to embrace this thing we call life
no, it is not
you can do it right where you are
right this minute
get outside, breathe, look at the trees
put your bare feet on the grass
hand on your heart to feel that pulse
and that's it

you're living, keep that up

wait up for the moon sometimes
or get up early to see a sunrise
just because you can
jump in the lake
run, skip, dance
the things you need to feel alive
are all around
you just have to see them

let in opportunity
and say yes to the invitations that scare you a little
in a good way

say no to some of the things you force yourself to do
knowing they rinse you of your peace

life was never supposed to be a waiting room
it was supposed to be a hillside
with paths leading in every direction
and mountains as far as the eye can see
hiding adventures and new friends behind them

don't let yourself get to the end of this ride
without having stopped to smell those beautiful roses
that's the only thing you need to fear in this life
everything else is all part of it

it's all just a messy, complicated, beautiful
and terrifying part of it

chin up, throw your arms wide open
and let it be so.

"If you
linger in the
past too long
your story
cannot
unfold
the way
it should"

THE EDGE

Standing at the edge of a new chapter can be scary. The desire to run back into the pages you know so well is more than tempting. But you must keep moving. Chapters end, even the good ones. And if you linger in the past too long, your story cannot unfold the way it should. And you might just miss the most beautiful moments of your life, whilst grieving the ones gone by. It's scary at the edge, my friend, I know. But just jump. You have so much ahead. And the good stuff behind, will always be there.

WOMEN

In this life we women are many things
mothers, sisters, wives, friends, carers

we are creators
we are nurture
we are *home*

but above all
we women are the magic
we are the intuition

we are the product of generations
who fought to be heard
to be believed
to be empowered

and that runs very deep

when women come together
magic happens, my friend

and those who tell you otherwise are afraid

we are not

so come together in all your glory when
you can
because you can
because you *must*
because you are called by deep-seated
ancestry to do so

and because, most of all
we hold up half the sky
and our half must show the other

how to *be*.

"We should
be allowing
ourselves to
consistently
expand
to grow"

CONFETTI

We spend our lives trying to be smaller. Trying to shrink our bodies so we don't overstep some invisible boundary of *too much person*. And I think that shrinking doesn't end with our flesh, either. We constantly hone, tone and downsize ourselves. When maybe, perhaps, we should be allowing ourselves to consistently expand, to grow. Imagine getting to the end and thinking, *I didn't offend anyone with my messy everything-ness*, when we could be looking back and seeing how we rained joy upon this planet, like a lorry load of love-filled, chaotic confetti.

YELLOW

Some people walk into your life with a light
that can only be described as *yellow*

infusing the very air around with the silent sound
of *this will be okay*
nothing hard can stay
we will find a way
together
we can reach calmer weather

these people, your *yellows*
are sunny, endlessly funny
they are warm and safe
a comforting place

they're a light things can grow in
their heart they wholly throw in
they are cheerleaders for your win

and if you have a *yellow* in this life
keep them bright
they thrive on giving out light
but they fight
their own dark too

they need a color beside them
to push on through

and I think they found a fellow *yellow*
in you.

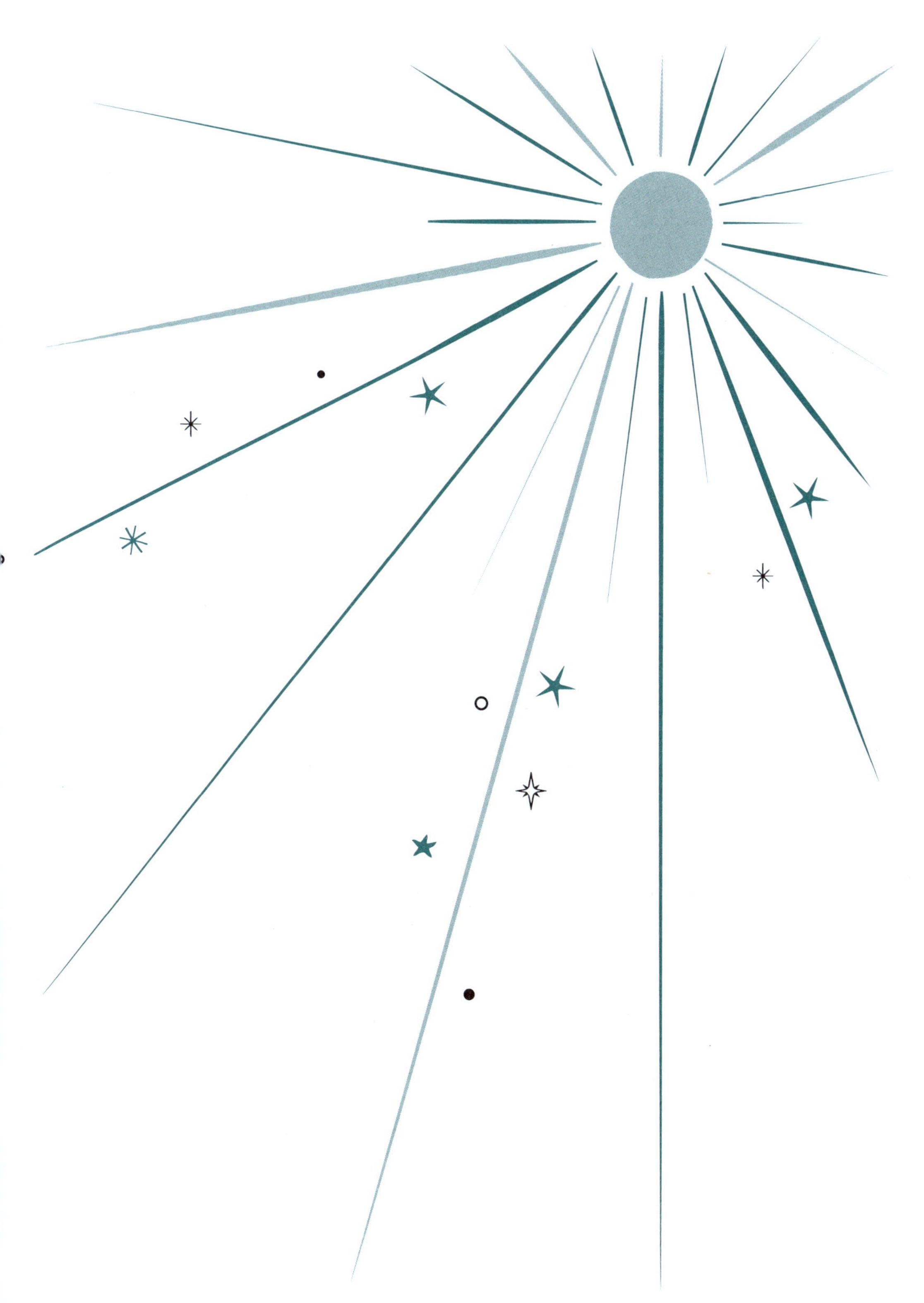

"Your light
is simply
made of the
you-ness
that makes
you *you*"

YOUR LIGHT

Your light does not come from your success
your light is not ignited by perfection
or achievement
or body shape

your light is not fueled by popularity or acceptance
neither is your light at any risk of being put out
when other lights around you are bright

your light is simply made of the you-ness
that makes you *you*
the worries you have in the night
the music which sparks your joy
the books you had to read twice
the memories stored safely in your heart
the people you love and the people who love you

your light is never dependent on how you look
or how you perform
it's just there
and it's quite simply brilliant
and it's all yours

and it lights up every room you walk into
whether you activate it or not

what a wonderful thing

shine bright, little fighter
this dark world needs your glow.

"You must
make sure joy
stays high
in the mix"

LET JOY STAY HIGH

If you have a chance
to let loose today
to unclench the safety bar
throw your hands
high in the air
take it

the world will always be a boiling pot
of good, bad and ugly

a confusing kaleidoscope
of all emotions at once

but you must make sure joy
stays high in the mix

joy, hope and love

these are the ones
that will keep the balance from
ever shifting downwards

so feel them
and wave them aloft
for others to see too

do not hide them away, my friends
they spread like wildfire
and the world needs that warmth.

"Wonderful
new people
who shine light
into your soul
will come
on in, if you
leave space"

YOU'LL BE OKAY

The one thing we know for sure, is that nothing lasts forever. In this journey, you will grieve. You will grieve people who are still alive, as well as those who have passed on. You will grieve shattered dreams, and you will grieve versions of yourself and others you had to break free from. But that's okay. In this life nothing lasts forever, but with that same truth comes the knowledge that all pain will lose its bite too. And great new things will emerge. Wonderful new people who shine light into your soul will come on in, if you leave space. And as long as you cry whenever you must, laugh whenever you can and love every day your little broken heart still beats, you will be okay. You will be more than okay.

LESS

To the woman
who may somehow feel less today
because she dropped a ball
missed a deadline
forgot something *important*
or failed to be all things to all people
in the most perfect of ways

you are not alone

everyone else felt that way today too
it's as common as a nose on a face
and it should cause you no shame
worry or regret

you will most likely
get things wrong again tomorrow
such is life

no one gets it just right
how could they
when it is not possible

you are a flawed
ball-dropping
wonderful human being
with a million intricate patterns
faults, flaws and foibles
intertwined so complexly
in your beautiful kaleidoscope soul

and so am I, how wonderful.

GREENER GRASS

The grass will often look greener elsewhere. And maybe it is, or maybe it's fake? Maybe that grass has been lovingly watered every day; maybe the weather has been just the perfect kind to grow that grass right. What I'm trying to say is, your grass is green enough. And if you water it more and shine some sunlight on it daily, it will only grow greener still. Love your own grass. Everything you love only gets better.

THE EMPTY NEST

My nest is as it should be now
empty

tidy, ordered
calm

my babies have grown, beautifully
and flown
just the way I taught them to

and my heart is full of pride, and love
still so full of love

but oh there is an ache there
a throb, a pang
I have given of myself in a way
that only a mother can
so consuming is that gift
there is scarce room
for much else to thrive

so what now?

my empty nest feels hollow
the echo of my own breath
rings in my ears

my worries have not flown
with the fledglings
they linger still
but now without the comfort

of a slumbering head
on a pillow upstairs

my imagination tells the tales
I don't want to see
and my spare time
once so coveted
is now my enemy

my nest is as it should be now
empty

but I will not be empty, little one
I will fly, just like you
find my new place in this story

play music, bring friends
make noise and laughter
and fill the house with life
so that when you come home
you see nothing to worry about here
for that may clip
your beautiful wings

and you will remember
how nurturing your nest once was
and you will crave the feeling of it
just once in a while
this nest will never close
and nor will I let it lose its love

fly, my loves, fly
but remember the way back home.

"They are
disguises
and without
them, my
soul rises"

SPEAK LESS

I'm learning to speak less and say more. To come in from the cold through my own front door. Where I am safe. To know that home is not always a place. It can also be skin. After all, it is the place you spend all your life within. And I am trying to think less and *be more*. To judge less and lose score. In this game. I'm no longer attached to the blame. I let it slip away alongside shame. Yes, I am learning, that these things for which I've spent my whole life yearning, are not prizes. They are disguises. And without them, my soul rises.

WISE OLD WOMAN

I once met a wise old woman
whose face spoke
of many hard years

she was eager to part me her wisdom
and her words surely moved me
to tears

put it down
she said with great passion
that load that
you're carrying there
it was only supposed to be fleeting
but you've borne it for all
these long years

which load? I inquired with surprise
for my hands were as
empty as air

she placed her hand straight on my heart
it's the load that you have
right in there

let it go now, my child, and be free
don't wear yourself thin
like I did

it's okay to drop it and leave it
place it down now
go out and live.

ANGELS

I like to think angels pull souls from bodies
before pain and tragedy strike

safe from harm in loving arms

pressing eyes and ears against soft wing
so they know no earthly suffering

only love, only safety, only peace
I think, no matter how they leave

they are protected as they go

and whilst this act I cannot prove
just like I can't explain to you
the invisible power of hope or love
or the magic of seeking solace in beliefs

I feel it makes some sense of grief

just like I feel
no, I *know*, that it's real

that people live on
never leaving us alone

long after the angels
lift us up and take us home.

SPRING

I have always believed spring to be the harbinger of hope, the launch pad to lighter days, the gateway to life. Spring soothes our winter-worn souls with anticipation, and its promise of more. It gently shakes our hibernating toes and whispers, *wake now, your wintering days are done.* And so, with each eager sunrise, we emerge, we reignite, we re-energize. And as with the nature around us, we begin to rise and renew. Come on in, spring, we have much longed for your light, for your joy, for your *new*. We are slowly rousing from slumber, welcome back.

SUMMER

Summertime, when the living is easy. When life is at its bountiful peak and days are so deliciously long, there is no end to the promise they hold. Summer is the time to be alive, to make hay whilst the sun shines and to fill your energy stores with memories of joy, which will fill the otherwise empty hearths of your heart with fire, all winter long. Do not let worries or fears stop you from embracing the sun, the *joy* you so deserve, my friends. You are gifted many summers in your life, but never quite enough. You deserve to *live* them. To feel them. Summertime, when the living is easy, so live easy.

"Autumn
does not
shudder at
the thought
of winter
ahead"

AUTUMN

Most rejoice at the sight of spring, but I have always loved autumn. Rich, righteous colours, a shedding of weight and submission to a force larger than you. The revelation of one's true self. Bare and unafraid. Warmed and dressed not by folly, but by innate wisdom. And the *knowing*, that this is as it must be and *everything will pass*. Autumn does not shudder at the thought of winter ahead; it peacefully basks in the last of the sun, counting every moment as a blessing and a vital part of the journey. It lets its leaves fall to the ground to nurture the new, like droplets of nourishing gold, and finds peace where no peace existed before. I've always loved autumn. It's the letting go, you see. Let it *go*.

WINTERING

You may think yourself lazy, or flawed. Yet your body is made of almost exactly the same elements as the stars. Your bone composition matches perfectly the coral in the seas, and you, my friend, are ruled by the moon and the sun, the tides and the planets. Whether you like it or not. So, no, you are not *lazy*, you are not *late*. Nature is simply pulling you to slow, like the life, flora and fauna around you. It is not your moment to rise. Look around you. It is winter. You are *wintering*. And you are right on time.

JOY COMES BACK

When you finally realize

that joy is less fireworks, more firefly
less orchestra, more birdsong

she will come back much more often

for joy will not fight
with the fast pace of this life
she dallies not in the shiny or the new

she breathes in the basic
shimmers in the simple
and dances in the daily to and fro

joy has been beckoning you
for many a year, my friend
you were just too busy doing, to see

the very next time joy wraps
her quiet warmth around you
as the garden embraces
your weary body in its wildness

tip her a nod
you cannot force her to stay
but if you are a gracious host

joy comes back.

"When the
world seems
bad, remember
most people
are **good**"

GOOD

Most people are good. Most people kiss their pets goodbye and read *just one more* bedtime story to their children. Most people visit their grandparents even when they have no time and stop by to check on quiet friends after a long day. Most people return their shopping trolleys, despite being already late, and let someone with only one item jump to the front of a queue. Most people give money when money is scarce and most people worry about people they don't even know, day in and day out. When the world seems bad, remember, most people are **good**.

"You are
capturing
this life
as it
happens"

THE TAKER OF THE PHOTO

I am the taker of the photos
I am the receiver of the groans
eye-rolls and *hurry ups*
I am the one who disrupts the *moments*
to capture them
but I am also the holder of the memories

I am the holder of the stories
I am the one who keeps the precious proof
and if you are too
please know
you are capturing this life
as it happens

capturing stages, ages, twists, turns
and last moments
no one could have foreseen

generations to come
will thank you for this
even if no one does right now

the eye-rolls will be replaced one day
with absolute all-consuming gratitude
for the image of a smiling face so missed
and a memory returned home to stay

keep disrupting life to capture it
when it's all that is left
someone, somewhere
will be so very glad you did.

"Don't be
fooled
beautiful
one, you are
not here to
preserve"

PRECIOUS

This world wants you to spend your precious time and money fighting the aging process and desperately trying not to take up too much space, when you could be spending both on adventures, new experiences and spiritual journeys. All of which you will share with your loved ones, inspiring generations to come. Don't be fooled, beautiful one, you are not here to preserve, to mummify yourself in life. You are here to live. It's your stories, your advice and your love that will last long after your death. Your body has a shelf life, but your soul does not. Wear your body out, in the most beautiful ways. It was always meant to be so.

IN REST, THEY REMEMBER

Some people are slowly taken
to the other realm
not physically, but mentally
memory by memory
they are pulled from us
like a painstakingly slow house-move

boxes full of life
chapters, people, loves
all packed into a van
to await their arrival on the other side

and as these parts are removed
those left feel lonelier daily
as though their love is already leaving them

it is a painful departure, my friends
this much is sadly true

but I like to think of the person we knew
reaching the other side, *finally*
once more *whole*
and upon arrival they see their boxes
awaiting them so long
they open them up
the chapters, the memories, the loves
and reunite with them all again

I can feel that heartfelt joy
and it brings me joy too
they are not lost for long
though it may feel so
in rest
they remember it all.

FEATHERS

I left you a little white feather
I placed it right there in your way
I wrapped it in love with a message
to let you know you'll be okay

I drew you a colorful rainbow
it followed your car for a while
I made a spectacular rainbow
I hoped it would show me your smile

I flew down a beautiful robin
it landed right there on your ledge
I prayed he would give you the strength
to push yourself back from the edge

I dropped you a shiny old penny
smoothed by the passing of time
I hoped you would keep it forever
the same way your soul's linked with mine

I try every day to remind you
that I never did go away
the feathers, the rainbows, the robins
are my way of trying to stay.

Every day

in

some

small way

it is

already *here*

ALREADY HERE

I know you think it's not coming for you, the joy. I know you believe you are not here to receive. That you are broken, not chosen, left naked and frozen. *All that good stuff is for others*, you say. And yet, I see when you *feel*. I *know* that you *know* these statements are not real. I saw you close your eyes, head raised to the sunlight. Saw you flirting with the moon on those balmy summer nights. Saw you laugh with true abandon, saw you let go to the random. I saw you take what life creates. You just didn't see what it was that you ate. It's not too late. It's not coming for you, my love, it is not near. Every day, in some small way, it is already *here*.

LOVE DOESN'T START WITH A SHOE

Love doesn't live in a diamond
or a candlelit dinner for two
love isn't just like the fairytale
love doesn't start with a shoe

love doesn't need any money
or a holiday in the sun
love doesn't come with conditions
or depend on the joy and the fun

love comes in everyday moments
like a text to say *thinking of you*
love is the call in the morning
to give you the will to push through

love is the listening to worries
and giving your problems an ear
love is the not giving up
love is the need to be near

love isn't always romantic
it's shouty, ugly and true
it's the breaking and growing together
love doesn't start with a shoe.

"Sunday is
your gift
your day to
recharge
your
freedom"

TOO MANY SUNDAYS

Too many Sundays have been darkened by the dreaded presence of Monday, looming in like a storm cloud of fear, anxiety and gut-wrenching stress. Sunday is your gift, your day to recharge, your freedom. Be protective of that time. Monday has its space enough; do not let it overstep its mark. Make your plans, prepare, then push Monday back into its box and let Sunday shine forth like the jewel it is. You deserve this day of soul rest. Life is not a chore to be dealt with; it's to be lived, my friend. You're here to *live*. And Sunday is a day, gifted to us, for doing whatever your little heart desires.

WILD

Keep a little bit of you wild, child

that little part of you that seeks out the moon
the sunrise, the waterfalls

the part of you that craves the freshest of air
the thickest of forests and the giant waves

it's important

for she is directly connected
to the core of the earth
the tides and the stars
she's intrinsically linked to all creation
to life itself, to existence

don't let the modern world push her out

she is wild and she is free
and you need her, to be the you
you were always meant to be

keep a little bit of you wild, child

just a little bit.

"There the
moon will
be, shining
through the
dark and
reminding
you you're
not alone"

ECLIPSE OF GRIEF

Maybe grief is the moon and love is the sun. And as they pass one another into the unknown, there is a kind of mystical eclipse. The grief blocks out all the light, you see. All the love, all the everything. I know. But that can't last. They will shift into their new places eventually. And whilst they dance this heart-breaking waltz, it is vital that you don't forget how to breathe. That's it. That's all you need to be alive... a heartbeat and a breath. And if you sit there, with those life-givers, hope will find you, every day. Just a little. And joy may even sneak in too. Through the cracks. Fleetingly. Let them. Because one day the moon will anchor firmly in place amongst the stars and let the sun beat down again in all her glory. And you deserve that light. And every night, there the moon will be, shining through the dark and reminding you you're not alone. Until it's time for you to finally come home.

WHEN WE'RE OLDER

When we're older let's meet every Sunday at four
in that cute little café we love
let's laugh at our foibles, our mishaps and then
release our mistakes to above

we can share a new wrinkle, a hair that's turned gray
and marvel at how we have grown
we can both reminisce on the lives that we've led
and be grateful for each day we've known

when we're older let's meet by that tree in the park
the one where the blossom grows yearly
we can share what we have and toast with a drink
remembering those we loved dearly

we will not give a thought to the youth we have lost
for we see so much worth in the change
we won't feel the rush of a fast-ticking clock
for we know time is ours to arrange

when we're older, let's meet every Sunday at four
in that cute little café we love
let's be wowed by how we have weathered this life
let's release our regrets to above.

"But you should
make it very much
your business
to like
yourself"

NONE OF YOUR BUSINESS

You could wake up today and make it absolutely none of your business who likes you and who doesn't. Just as you care very little for whether someone likes coffee or prefers tea. Because in your life there will be a veritable mix of the coffee and tea drinkers, and none of that will be the fault of the bean or the leaf. You should make it none of your business who likes you and who doesn't. But you should make it very much your business, to like yourself. And let those you like, know it. *Then, enjoy your coffee, let them enjoy their tea. In this world of all things, where acceptance is free.*

AS TIME GOES BY

As time goes by
you will loosen your grip on that rock
the one you always thought was home
and you will realize that home is not a place
it's a state of mind
let it go

as times goes by
you will learn to see yourself more clearly
the girl who was always too much of one thing
and too little of another, was actually
everything she needed to be
let her out

as time goes by
you will let the simple things become the big
and you will allow the big things to become the simple

and that readjustment will be
the day you really start to live
let it be

as time goes by
you will be forced to say goodbye many times
and your soft little heart will shatter, but
it will still beat, and that will bring you
all the purpose you need
let it beat

as time goes by
you will stop choosing wealth over peace
you will stop choosing money over time
and you will see that the treasures you need
are in the smiles and the laughter
let them in

as times goes by
the moments you remember when your life flashes past
are never the awful memories, my friend, it's the joy
the summer nights, the lazy days with loved ones
the midnight chats and the morning hugs
let them happen

let them all happen.

“Do you get
how bold
it is to be
wildly alive
when the
world insists
you must
just survive
instead?”

THIS LITTLE MOMENT

Do you see how courageous it is to live in this little moment, when lists itch to be ticked? Do you know how brave you are to drop tasks in favor of a friend who beckons you to play? Or a moment with your child that may never come around quite the same again? Do you get how bold it is to be wildly alive when the world insists you must just survive instead? My friends, allow the garden to pull you in for a breath of pure oxygen. Linger with the last gasps of the sun tonight. Or let the moon beckon you from all that doing, to just being. Be outrageously courageous and just exist for a moment. Just for this one little moment.

FRIENDSHIPS

I don't think friendships
are given enough credit

we sign no contract
we say no vows
and yet we are there for each other

for better or for worse
in sickness and in health

we laugh together
in life-giving amounts
we cry together
without shame

we pull each other up
out of the mud
again
and again
and again

I don't think friendships
are given enough credit

unwritten love stories
each and every one.

I HAVE BEEN HER

I have been her
I have been she
I have been them
and now I'm me

I have been out
and I've been in
I've felt defeat
I've known the win

I have held joy
and shouldered grief
I've had my share
of changed beliefs

I have been hurt
and I've been high
I found no answers
to what and why

I know the loss
and I know the gain
I know that we
all bleed the same

I have been her
I have been she
I have been them
and now I'm *me.*

STOP

The world won't stop still if you do
the tides will not cease to flow
the sun will still rise and set if
you take some time out alone

the sky will still rumble if you rest
the days will still move into night
the world will continue to turn if
your fire needs time to ignite

the people will breathe still without you
the chores will stay patiently there
the things on your list will not wander
if you take time out for self-care

the world won't stop still if you do
so fear not the tears in your eyes
they wash and they clear up your vision
and that's how you reset and rise.

"You were able to keep safe a special shiny nugget of your true self"

A LITTLE WEIRD

May you forever remain a little weird. Because what that really means is you were able to keep safe a special shiny nugget of your true self from a world that tried so hard to bash it out. And I think that somebody, somewhere along the way must have loved you enough so you recognized that treasure for what it was. And if they didn't, then even more kudos to you for giving that gift to yourself. May you forever remain a little weird and completely, entirely you.

FORGOTTEN GRAVY

I love imperfectly mismatched rooms
homemade decorations
and trinkets
that tell stories of the past

I treasure impromptu gatherings
with food rustled up from nowhere
it's always just *enough*

I see the beauty in gifts handed over
with words of *oh it's nothing*
for that simply means the giver
cannot begin to convey
how they really feel about you

I value both the quiet moments
when the lights twinkle privately
and the raucous occasions
when laughter fills the room

and I can't get enough of burnt carrots
forgotten gravy
and failed attempts at dessert

because that's where the love lives
in the imperfect
in the messy
in the real

love lives in the forgotten gravy
look for it.

OR YOU COULD JUST LIVE . .

You are going to wish your body was more
you are going to wish your body was less
you are going to wish your body would change
you are going to wish your body would not

you are going to wish your body was many things
between now
and the day you leave this mortal coil

and one day
as is always the way
you will look back
and see
that your body was always as it should be
doing its best
to be you
for you

and you are then going to wish that just once
you had told your body
I accept you, as you are, right now

and that maybe, had you done this
you would have spared yourself a lifetime
of wishing for something you didn't really ever need

that what it was you should have been wishing for, in fact
was the courage to accept
the strength to embrace
the wisdom to really see
what you *have*.

"She simply
stopped
fighting time
stopped
fighting
nature"

SHE LET HERSELF GO

She let herself go, they say

how wrong they are, how little they know
she simply stopped fighting time
stopped fighting nature
and ceased being a slave
to the unreachable dictations of society
she focused instead on the real things
pressing for her attention

she let herself in
she let herself rest
she let herself be
she let herself out
at no point did she let herself go
quite the opposite
if only they could see it

if only they could do it too.

"It is but
a beat in
this magical
masterpiece"

ZOOM IN

In a hundred years, none of us will be here. We'll all be back to the earth that grew us, or dispersed amongst the stars which imploded so long ago to give us the building blocks we needed to make this life. And if you have any faith at all in the unexplainable, there we will be. Wondering what all the fuss was about. Wondering why we gave away years of living when we were supposed to use the pain to hyper-focus on the moment. Hyper-focus if you can. Zoom in on the details. Get right up in the face of this gift we are given, because it is but a beat in this magical masterpiece. One century out of 45 million so far. Zoom in. Be here. Let go.

TO THE WOMAN WHO HAS GIVEN TOO MUCH

To the woman who has given too much
to the woman who has taken too much
to the woman who has no idea
how she will keep going like this
every day

I see you

I see how exhausted you are
I see your desire to run for the hills
without a care in the world

and I know that if you did so
the world which you have created
would collapse
without you
so, of course
that is not an option

and I know
just how oppressive the weight of that can be
how suffocating it is
how scary that feels sometimes

and I also know
how *grateful* you are for this load you carry
for it's everything you need
and yet all that consumes you
and that's okay

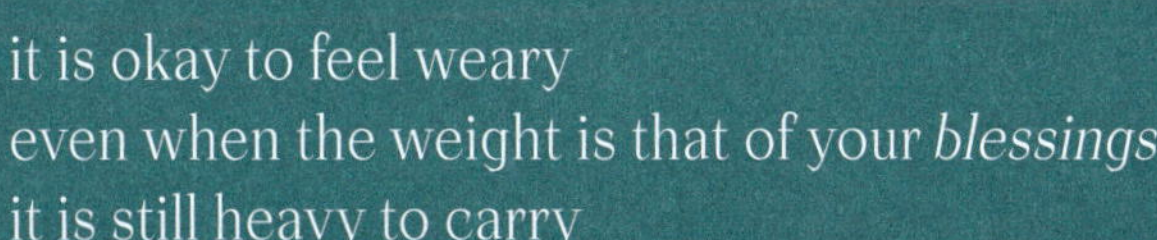

it is okay to feel weary
even when the weight is that of your *blessings*
it is still heavy to carry

there is no space for shame
in that load of yours
no space for guilt
no space for perfection
set those down

lighten your load of those things

next, take out the need
to conform to others' expectations
and gather up all the past mistakes
and the worries for the future

they can all go

lastly, the spaces you have just made
should be filled with rest
for we know that resting is very much doing
and then add in your joy
and whatever space is left
leave it there

ready for new things
things which will show up
as soon as they see their space waiting
it's high time they did.

When you

can find

joy

in the

mundane

life opens *up*

SMALL JOYS

If life feels draining and heavy right now, celebrate the small joys. I mean the really small joys. When the morning radio plays your kind of music and the toast is crisped perfectly. When the parcel arrives on time and the washing dries outside. When your sheets feel cool and crisp and your friend texts to say they are thinking of you. Quietly celebrate the heck out of all those tiny things and you will find your joy in the mundane. And when you can find joy in the mundane, life opens up, perspective shifts and beauty reveals itself to you ...from all around.

"A day is only
lost if you
forgot to say
something kind
to yourself
or another"

A DAY IS NOT LOST

A day is not lost
if you failed to tick off a list
or a diet was broken

a day is only lost
if you forgot
to say something kind
to yourself
or another

if you forgot
to pause
to search
for a tiny spark of beauty
amongst the drudgery
glimmering like gold
in the mud

a day is only lost
if you forgot
that life
even in the worst of times
is still a *gift*
a gift you so very much deserve
to *live* through

and not just **survive**.

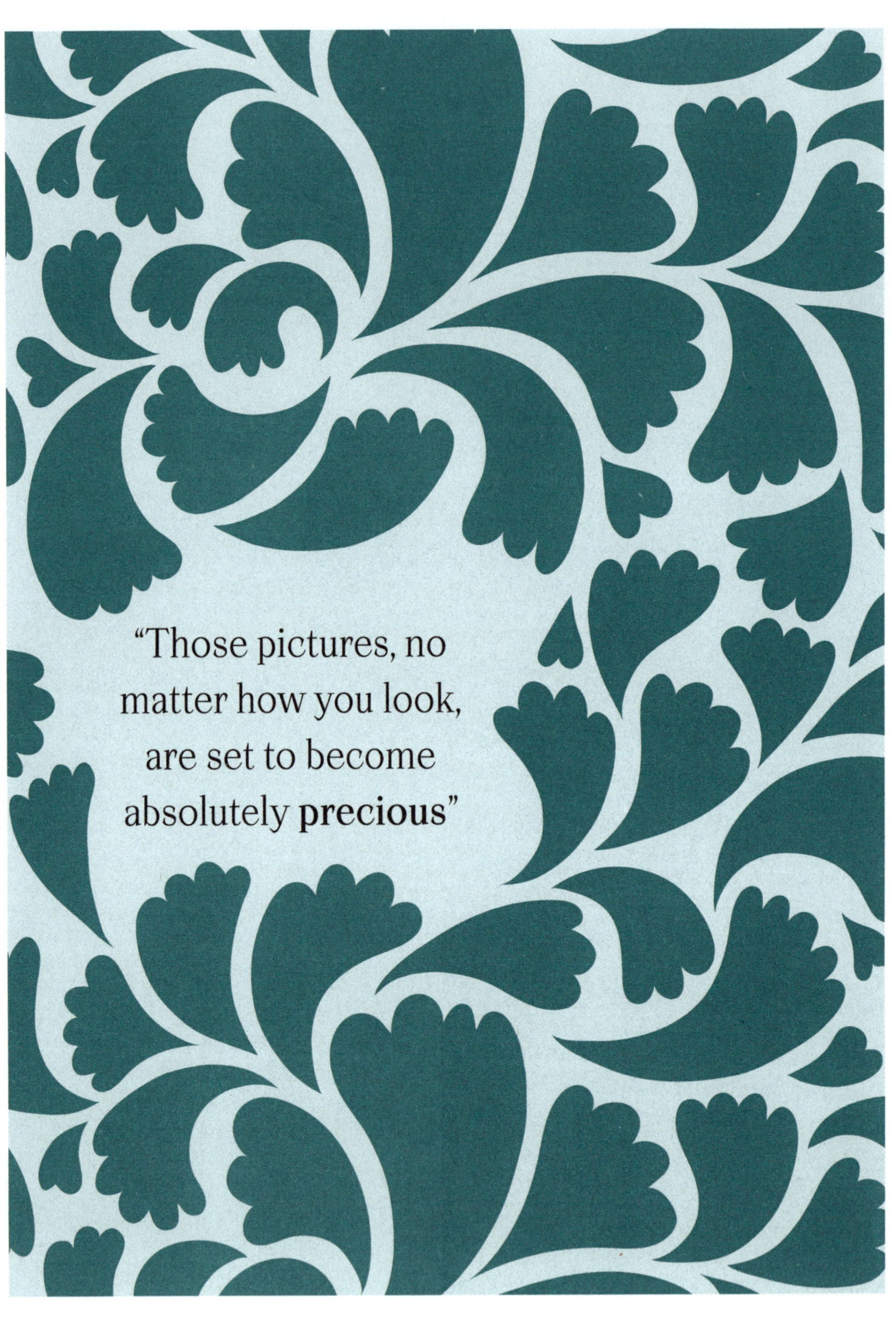
"Those pictures, no
matter how you look,
are set to become
absolutely **precious**"

IN THE PHOTO

It's easy to shy away from photographs because you're so busy, so exhausted, not feeling your best. It's easy to be the *taker* and never let yourself be in, when holidays make you feel exposed or *less than*. But one day, your loved ones will search for those memories to bolster their own. Those pictures, no matter how you look, are set to become absolutely **precious**. And no one, not one of them, will care how *together* you appear. They will care, very much, that it is *you*. And all of your *you-ness* will be the exact gift they very much need in that moment. Be in the photo, my friends. *They are not for you.*

A MOTHER'S LOVE

A mother's love
lives in the gut
deep
deep within the gut

deep down
where the soul shakes hands with instinct
where the present day combines
with intuition honed by ancestors

that's where a mother's love lives

a mother's love is fierce
primal
cellular
built-in
everlasting
mountain-moving
barrier-breaking
standard-shaking

if you dare to challenge
this age-old energy
prepare to witness
humanity
at its strongest

there is nothing more
nothing *deeper*
than a mother's love.

WILDLINGS

This goes out to the mamas
raising the wild ones
the *not to be tamed*
the rare
the reckless
and the *precious*

you are shaping stardust
into human form
minding moonlight
till it's ready to instruct the tides
and light the nights

do not expect the world to see
your diamond in the rough
sparkle
not yet
they cannot

but one day
they will be unable
to take their eyes away
from its shine

to the mamas of the wild ones
you are star gatherers
moon catchers
and dream shapers

and you are exhausted

but shaping starlight
into human form
was always going to be tough
and you are.

"All this talk
of women
having
gone mad
is actually
just women
waking up"

AWAKENING

The older I get, the more I realize that all this talk of women having gone mad is actually just women waking up one day, smelling the coffee and feeling furious. Furious that they twisted themselves like a pretzel all these years trying to conform to what others wanted them to be. Furious that they didn't say *no* more, or - more to the point - that they didn't say *hell no* more. Furious that they didn't say *yes* more, that they didn't feel they could put themselves first. Furious that their feelings, their emotions and their desires were branded as hormonal all these years, as a lame excuse to fob them off and not face up to bad behavior. And no, this is not just the menopause. This is called awakening. The older I get the more I realize that women are not going mad. In fact, they are becoming very sane indeed.

ROOTS OF SISTERHOOD

When women root together we grow taller
even though the soil we get
was made for smaller
it is an energy thing; what we take, we bring
and when our soil is crowded
we simply move everything
to make space, to let another female root
with grace

our branches twist and curl
but never smother
they twine and thrive alongside one another
reaching for light, and all that is right
never blocking out the sun
always thinking of someone

and when the world turns dark
and we must shed
we bravely bare, by nature, we are led
this forest filled with trees of every hue
a place for me to bloom alongside you

and always, wisdom glowing
as this multiverse keeps growing
taking nutrients and sharing what we're sowing
when women root together, we grow wilder
as we show each newborn seed
just what's inside her.

"You are
already
enough
but reaching
for more is
your right"

YOU JUST GREW

It is brave to want to be better
braver still to understand
that you are already enough
but reaching for more is your right
you are a seed instructed by light
not a creature of the night
and if the other flowers in your field
do not support the way you grow
let them go
all they truly need to know
is that you are brave to want new
you are nature
you just grew
and that's okay
you did not come here to stay

let old leaves fall away.

"What if
you stopped
that from
happening
right here
right now?"

RIGHT NOW

What if you get to the end of your life and you suddenly make the connection, that you were supposed to enjoy it? That you were supposed to let go and live, make stories to pass on, because material possessions don't bring half as much joy as the memories of love that you leave? What if you realize, too late, that your cellulite and tummy rolls were adorable, actually, and should never, ever, have been enough to stop you having fun? What if your last thoughts were regrets for not enjoying this ride, and giving it all that you had? What if you stopped that from happening, right here, right now? What if...?

WHEN FIREWORKS FALL

When you're just too tired to sleep
and your pillow feels like lead
when the worries in your mind
fly like fireworks in your head
when your bones are made of metal
and your muscles loathe to move
and your heart is numb and far too full
of this world's ugly truths

on these nights when you can't settle
and the planet seems so cold
let me walk amongst those fireworks
let me be the one who's bold
I will catch them in my hands
and pop them safe beneath your bed
I will leave some lovely thoughts
to fly around in there instead

when your body won't continue
and your soul just needs a break
don't forget I'm always here
and I will gladly be your brave
you're not alive to be alone
so let me catch you when you stall
and I promise I will let you catch me too
when fireworks fall.

FRIEND SHIP

I like to think a friendship is just that: a ship. Some are built to last. Made to navigate any ocean, whatever the weather. Perfect for feeling the breeze in your hair, seeking exciting new adventures and seeing life at its lightest. But strong enough to navigate the changing tides, the rising storms and the roughest of hosting seas. If friendship is a ship, and friends are crewmates - then I am glad, so glad, you are mine. We built her well, this ship of ours. We built her out of laughter, loyalty and, most of all, love. And she will carry us safely, I think. Right to the very end of our worldly adventures. And perhaps, I suspect, even after that.

FEATHERS THAT FLEW

On the day that you must lay me to rest
wear your best

it matters not if it's yellow or pink
there will simply not be time
to consider what people may think

you have laughing to do
all that fun we knew
and you know I always loved your shoes

save your blues

bring your brights

we will walk again in sunlight
and until that time arrives

I shall remind you loud and clear
that I'm still here

with things I found around the sky
like rainbows and moonbeams
and feathers that fly

to find your hand
be sure to understand
that this is my hello
I didn't truly go

I'm just beyond a wall but worry not
I can hear you call

and I call too

with rainbows and moonbeams
and feathers that flew.

BE KIND TO YOURSELF TOO

You're only a kind person
if you're kind to yourself too
otherwise you've fallen
into the people-pleasing trap
and that will break your spirit

kindness starts at home
and home starts with you
and you deserve that kindness
as much as any other

do not throw your kindness
out into this world
without gifting some of it your way

there is a little version of you
who waits deep inside
hoping for it
thirsty for that kindness

and they cannot accept it from others
until they feel worthy enough
and worthy starts at home too
worthy starts with you

you're only a kind person
if you're kind to yourself too

be kind to yourself too.

MAGICALLY SO

If you shine approval on someone
they flower
it's science
kind of magically so

if you consistently tell someone
they are wonderfully unique
they will believe it
and consequently
the world will believe it too
for that person will go forth
displaying their uniqueness
as the gift it truly is

so, stop telling the world all that you are not
and start showing them all that you *are*

expect that they will see the wonderful parts of you
because they will
if *you* do

celebrate your differences, my friend
and make them even more beautiful
with the power of your acceptance

even better
your approval

it's science,
kind of magically so.

You will

handle it all

because

that's what

you *do*

JUST A DAY

No, today probably won't be a great day, but it absolutely won't be a bad day either. Today will simply be a day. Twenty-four hours of a little bit of everything. Some moments will be hard, some will be joyous, some will be peaceful and some will be draining. And you, you will handle it all, because that's what you *do*. Don't put pressure on yourself to have any kind of a day, my friend. Life throws enough at you. Instead, just remind yourself that whatever happens, you are ready. And most importantly, you have your own back. It's just a day. Another day of life in all its messy everything-ness. **Lucky us.**

SADNESS COMES

Sadness came to tea last night
as she's often done before
but I didn't let her in this time
I stopped her at the door

I'm off to meet with friends, I said
your timing isn't right
I can't allow your atmosphere
it's not the place tonight

but sadness would not take the hint
her manners lack finesse
her pace was slow and heavy
yet she kept up nonetheless

and even when I took my seat
amongst my laughing friends
she squeezed herself right in between
her boldness never ends

and I was sure my friends would loathe
this specter at the feast
and somehow think me lesser
for inviting such a beast

but no, their warmth was undeterred
as if nothing was askew
I think perhaps they know by now
I sometimes come as two

and even sadness seemed to glow
a lighter shade of gray
to know that she's accepted
seemed to lighten up her day

so let your sad accompany you
don't think her hard to bear
no need to face her all alone
just pull an extra chair.

ONLY YOU

Only you will ever know the real you

everyone else sees a version of you
a version created in their mind
through their filters
using their own
experiences and judgments
to mold you

you may think they see
what you know
about yourself
but they don't

everyone you have ever met
holds a version of you
in their memory
none of them are real

it is a special moment
when this truth sinks in
because at last you realize
you've a very unique
thing going on
with yourself

so many versions of you exist
in very many places
but only you
will know the real one

now if that is not a relationship
well worth treasuring
what is?

“You feel so
much in so
many ways
every minute
of every day”

BEDFELLOWS

Anxiety, worry and fear are bedfellows we must live with, but that doesn't mean we have to let them take all the blankets. You are human, my friend, and that means you feel so much in so many ways, every minute of every day. You're not faulty; you're working as you should be. So, congratulate yourself on your ability to process the tsunami you seem to constantly face, and then tuck yourself into that bed with the negative emotions at the very bottom. They don't need to keep cozy and warm; you do.

GO LITTLE

When everything feels too big
go little

when the overwhelm
is dragging you down
go down

make yourself small
make your world small
wrap yourself in a blanket
and take every little task
one tiny crumb at a time

you can't outrun that tsunami
nor can you swim it

you must do as it wishes

let the wave wash you along
till finally
you open your eyes
on a beach
blinking at the sunlight
as it caresses your skin

when everything feels too big
go little.

"The sunrise
may be gone
today, but the
sunset is just
as beautiful, if
not more so"

THE CONCEPT OF AGE

Anti-aging as a concept is like trying to rewind the sunset every morning. It cannot be done. You are aging, every minute of every day. There is no way to reverse that; it is the fundamental journey of life. Why not get used to that now and start to enjoy the process, instead of dreading it and fighting? Believe me, there is much beauty you are missing. The sunrise may be gone today, but the sunset is just as beautiful, if not more so. And so are you. *So are you.*

SHE SENT

She sent me a book
with a page turned down
I barely had strength to read it
but I knew with my knowing
that she also knew
there was something in there
my heart needed

and as I began to take the words in
tears found their way to my cheeks
the lump in my throat let forth a soft howl
I'd been keeping inside for some weeks

like floodgates thrown open
a storm was released
a bottled-up genie set free
all of the magic I'd kept trapped inside
and all of those versions of me

she sent me a book
with a corner turned down
she sent me a key to my cage
all of her love and all of my pain
let loose
with the turn of a page.

"She floundered
so that I could find
peace today, every
misstep she took,
showed me
the way"

COFFEE WITH MY YOUNGER SELF

I met my younger self for coffee
and cake, and the bill was on me
because I owe that girl a lot
her nervous system for years, was shot
she floundered, so that I could find peace today
every misstep she took, showed me the way
she hated her skin so that I could be free
she grew through the concrete to let us be me
she suffered, yet the spoils are my prize
and despite all the fights and the lies
she is whole, always part of my soul
now, living as one is the goal
she took many hits and she broke into shards
but her heart never closed and she kept down
her guard
so that joy could sneak inside our skin
and I'm grateful, to the girl I was then.

"You won't
regret the things
you tried and
failed at but you
will regret a life
spent waiting"

THOSE WHO WAIT, WAIT

Waiting for anything is a dangerous game because there is no guarantee that conditions will ever be *just right*. If each of us knew how much time we had allocated, perhaps we could play around with it. But we don't. So waste time wisely, my friend. Time spent in rest, joy, company and kindness is never wasted. As for everything else, *just do it*. You won't regret the things you tried and failed at. But you will regret a life spent waiting. Those who wait, wait. You have a life to live.

YOUR PERFECT

If you are not broken
bruised
weathered
and worn
where have you been, my friend?

if your battered heart
does not still break
every day
then perhaps
you are not paying attention?

don't aim to come out of this life
preserved and perfect
you're supposed to crumble
and rebuild
a million times over
until your soul is satisfied
you have given your all

because that's why you are here

your perfect is not needed
but your broken
is very important

very important
indeed.

"It's
universal
like we're
at a huge
rehearsal"

OTHER GIRLS

I always wanted to be like the other girls, with perfect lashed eyes and bouncy curls. But I was destined to watch on, from rows behind. Waiting for some crumbs, on days they may be kind. I always wanted to be chosen first. No longer starving, mad with thirst. But now I see. That sometimes those girls wished they could be me. Free from the pressure of perfection, free to move in new directions, without care. For how the wind will ruin my hair. Nothing is fair. But we all have perfect eyes, and we all wear a disguise. It's universal. Like we're at a huge rehearsal. Until one day, we all reveal and we come together, being real. The other girls are me and I am them. And we wasted so much time not being friends.

THE WITCH WOUND

They call it the witch wound
we were *punished*, you see
broken, slain
for shining too brightly

so we learned to hide that spark
we learned to play it down
play dumb, play *dead*

and we were taught to fear
the light within us
lest it herald our downfall

but not *anymore*

you are not a witch, my friend
you are quite simply
or *complicatedly*
a woman

and your magic is not
something
you can choose, or lose
it always is
and always has
lived within you

and you need no longer hide it

they call it the witch wound
but the time to heal is here, *now*
let that magic out.

"It is a
thing of
great
beauty, an
ancient
duty"

THIS PLATONIC SONG

I learned. Many years before. That when my worth is on the floor, much of the romance I need will come from the platonic loves in my life, and not from husband to wife. And that's alright. Because women know. And that is neither excuse nor platitude; it comes from deep gratitude. We understand the neighborhood, you see. And we thrive, by helping one another survive, this rocky road of hormone-fueled life. It is a thing of great beauty, an ancient duty. And it is a love I very much rely upon. This platonic song. All along, it has been the grace that helped me take up much more space.

A HANDFUL OF YEARS

There will come a day
when you will glance
at your child
and be met by an adult

and it will wipe the very floor
from under your feet
when you realize
in that moment
that you were only ever minding them
until they fly away

because back then
when you were so consumed
with the daily grind of parenting
you felt like this was *forever*

yet we know
nothing truly is *forever*

just a handful of years
you will know them as a child
and if you are blessed
many more
you will know them as an adult

drink them in
if you can
drink them in.

"You will feel a
sense of utter
contentment
wash through
your bones and
dust your skin
with goose bumps"

FOREVER DAYS

There will be days that stick to the inside of your mind forever. Days that refuse to be forgotten, no matter what. And I think this is because these were days we got just right. This living. When we balanced the busyness with love. When we were present in body and spirit. Days when we reached out to invite others and reached in to invite ourselves too. Days when laughter and tears were both just as welcome and joy and sadness held hands beneath the table. Days where not much happened but actually, everything did. There will be days that become forever days, and they don't announce their arrival in advance, but at some point you will feel a sense of utter contentment wash through your bones and dust your skin with goose bumps... and that's when your soul takes a snapshot, and hangs it on the pinboard of your mind. To be gazed upon with fondness, forevermore.

I WISH I KNEW

I wish I knew from the start
that self-esteem is a home-grown virtue
and you must never plant those precious seeds
in someone else's garden

I wish I knew at every step
that all those seeds truly require
in order to bloom
is approval
from yourself

yes, I wish I knew way back then

that self-approval is their sunlight
peace is their soil and love is their rain

and all the other things can come and go
like the seasons and the wind
I wish I knew all along
that those seeds can grow so tall
so strong and so fierce
like the most beautiful sunflowers
if the conditions are right

or they can wither away to weed and husk
if neglected

I wish I knew a lifetime ago
that no matter how much of the world I
scoured
I would not find a better garden
than the one I could grow myself
if only I knew how

and I wish for you
to know this too
so you can grow
and water
you.

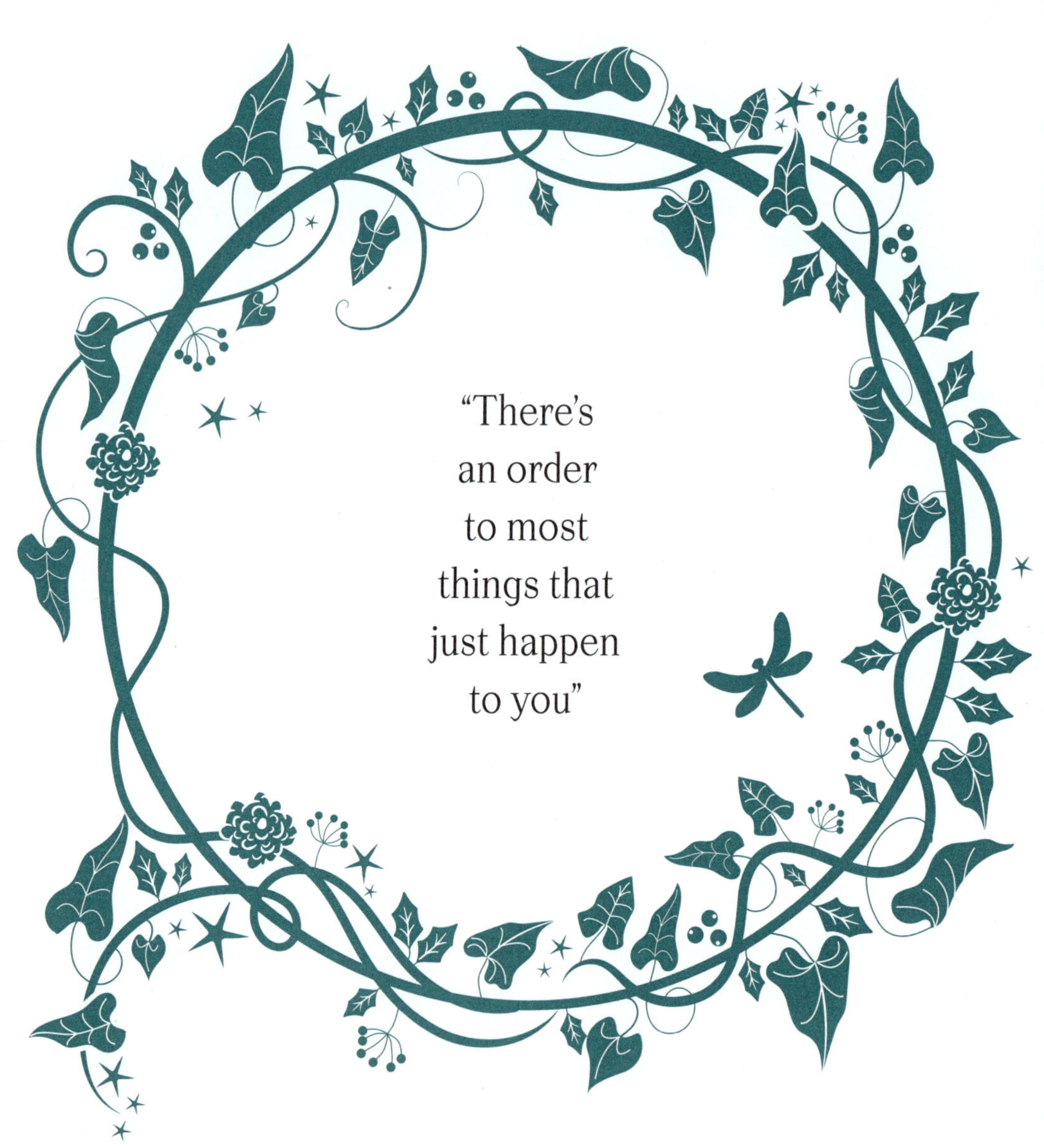

"There's
an order
to most
things that
just happen
to you"

SERENDIPITY

Random is rarely random. This much is true.
There's an order to most things that just happen
to you. Somewhere you knew. When the sign
blew your mind. When the page opened so freely
on the prose your soul chose. And the song that
made them teary, plays on days you hurt most.
Nothing is a shock, not really. And the more your
brain abandons to the random, the more light
siphons through. The more the signs can shimmy
their way over to you. You have to give up facts,
let the magic through the cracks, you see...
and make way, for soulful serendipity.

SPEAK YOUR LOVE

There are many things to fear in this life
but I have found that there is one
to be feared above all

the things you failed to say

always speak what is in your heart
always speak to those you love
as though that sentence
may be the last one you utter
because if it is
you will play those words over and over
and ache with every fiber of your being
to replace them with better
to replace them with *love*

to tell that person how magical
wondrous and joyous
they were
never fall into the trap of believing you have time
to speak your love
time is not something we can rely on

speak your love
every day
speak your love
come what may.

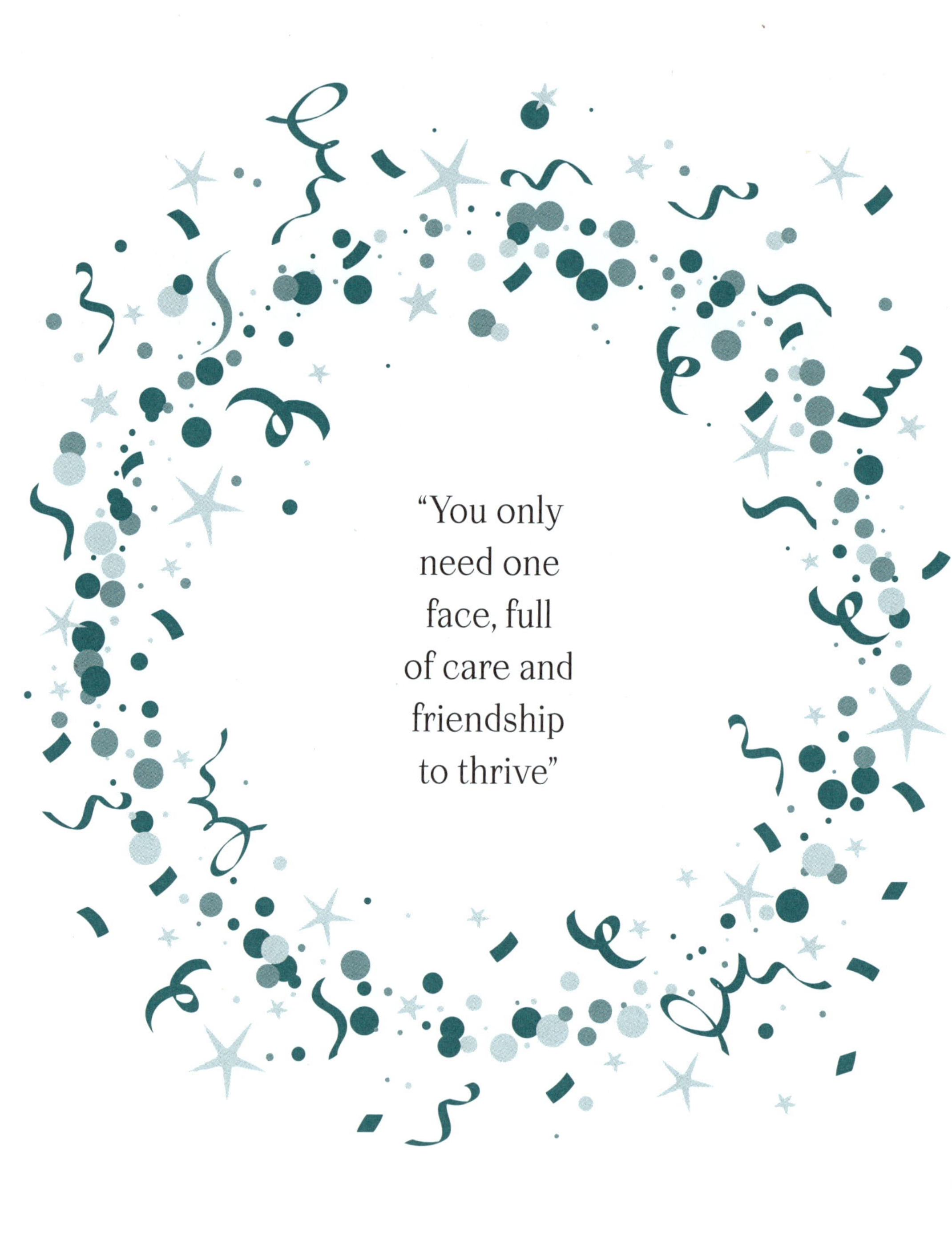

"You only
need one
face, full
of care and
friendship
to thrive"

THE AFTER-PARTY PEOPLE

Anyone can fill a room full of glittering people. Announce a party, send out invitations, bring food, wine, music and the promise of fun - they will come. But it is the after-party people you must treasure in this life. The ones who stay to help clear away. The ones who see you are exhausted from the organizing, and know you will need them then. The ones who call the day before and say, *What can I help you with?* despite being already overwhelmed in their own lives. The people who will show up for your house-move, for your worst days, for your *broken*. The people who stay when the show is over, the curtain has fallen heavily to the stage floor and the make-up is off. It is wonderful to be surrounded by fun-filled faces sometimes, but you only need one face, one little loving face, full of care and friendship, to thrive.

“The air
around me
fills with an
energy
that is life-
affirming
and joyful”

I WANT TO LISTEN

If you ever want to talk
about the person you are missing
I want to listen, *always*
and as you do this talking
they come alive again, for me
whether I knew them or not
your love, your stories
your picture painting of them works
and the air around me fills with an energy
that is life-affirming and joyful
I can't explain the science
but I can only assure you of the effect
it's real
they are real
and if you ever want to talk about them
in that energy effusive
enthusiastic way that you do
I want to listen.

ORDINARY LOVE

Some people love
in grandness
displaying that bright love
like a fountain of fiery romance
to rain flowers forevermore
upon the apple of their eye
telling the world
this love is *extraordinary*

and because this love
is so visibly majestic to behold
it is revered and desired
by those without it

but some people love
in ordinary
diligently and consistently
drip-feeding their love
in nurture form
often unseen or unnoticed
rarely celebrated
always reliable

and because this love
is so humble
it can be brushed away
as unimportant

yet without it

worlds would crumble
lives would fall apart
and souls would be forever seeking
their flamboyant mate

whilst passing by
their very cornerstone
right under the nose

I guess what I am trying to say is

there is no such thing as ordinary love
it is all quite amazingly
profoundly
extraordinary

whether it shouts from the rooftops
or whispers in the holding of a hand

you just have
to see it
to make it
the wondrous entity

you seek.

ROLLERCOASTER

This life is the biggest ride you'll ever go on
an
up
down
in
out
over
under
rollercoaster

the moments of joy
the *ups*
are truly technicoloured
let go of the bars
feel them
let them in

the moments of loss
the *downs*
are devastatingly terrifying
grab the bars tightly
feel them
ride it out

every day is a new twist and a new turn
but nothing
nothing
lasts forever

just as you think the worst part is here to stay
you slow down and catch the view
and it's a wonderful view

this life is the biggest ride you'll ever go on
let it be so.

"On the days
when your
anger is high
remember why"

LOVE CAME FIRST

You don't move on after loss, but you must move *with*. You must shake hands with grief, welcome her in, for she lives with you now. Pull her a chair at the table and offer her comfort. She is not the monster you first thought her to be. She is *love*. And she will walk with you now, *stay* with you now, peacefully. If you let her. And on the days when your anger is high, remember why she came, remember who she represents. *Remember*. Grief came to you, my friend, because love came first. *Love came first.*

You've done

that

beautifully

breaks

and all

LOST

You haven't lost yourself, my love

it's about knowing
what to look for in the mirror
you see

you won't find the old you in there
because you've *changed*
you've *evolved*
of *course* you have

that isn't a failure
that's an achievement

it's about finding the beauty in the new
instead of searching for the old

you haven't lost her
you've grown
as you were supposed to
and you've done that beautifully
breaks and all

there is much new beauty
you are simply not seeing

look again
with fresh eyes
there she is.

"You will
bruise reaching
out of your
comfort zone
and you will rot
staying inside it"

BRUISE

Finding a new garden in which to grow to full splendor is hard. But staying in barren soil will slowly kill you from the roots up. Taking a leap of faith requires a core of steel, but so does allowing your dreams to go out like a used match. Speaking your truth will make your knees knock and your voice tremble, but holding it in is an oil slick in a coral reef. Living life unmasked will leave you open, but that mask is cutting off your oxygen at the source, my love. The thing is, living is hard, but dying slowly is *hard* too. You will bruise reaching out of your comfort zone and you will rot staying inside it. This life, it will wound you every day and stitch you right back up again, if you are living it right. None of it is easy. Choose your bruise.

FOR A LIFETIME

If you plan to love someone for a lifetime
be prepared to grieve
for the versions of themselves
they will outgrow

if you plan to love someone for a lifetime
be prepared to fall in love anew
with the versions of themselves
they will grow into

and if you plan to *be loved*
for a lifetime
be ready to love yourself
in versions old and new

for only those who love within
can happily accept love

and as with everything
everything
in life
change is constant

and nothing stays the same.

SOUL TRIBE

You may think
that you do not have a tribe
because you never see them gather
but here's the thing
your tribe may gather in different ways
and you may not have their visual presence
but if you want to, if you wish to
you can feel their essence

close your eyes
and think of all the people who are for you
they adore you
and they may not be with you every day
but they show their tribal status
in many other ways
that's how soul tribes play

and if their numbers feel small
do not worry
it is not their number
it is their hurry
the way they rush to collect you
from the floor
when darkness knocks your door

from wherever they may be
they somehow see

and your tribe may never know one another
but the thing they have in common is you

so yes, you do have a tribe
and it lives within your soul
and it is you, just you
who makes that tribe whole.

"The invisible
net of love
laughter and
light you have
spread across
this planet"

THAT'S WHERE YOU FIND IT

You search for your beauty in the mirror, in photographs, in the label of clothes, when you really should be searching through the messages sent to you by grateful friends, the cards written to you on special days or in times of need, the memories of smiles you created from tears. Your beauty lies in all the ways you touch and care for those around you, my friend - the jokes you made on a gloomy day and the music you shared to inspire, the times you showed up when no one else did and the invisible net of love, laughter and light you have spread across this planet without glory or vanity. *That's* where you find your beauty.

"Remember
how they loved
you and do *that*
for yourself"

ON THOSE DAYS

On those days
when you miss someone the most

as though your memories
are sharp enough
to slice through skin and bone

remember how they loved you

remember how they loved you
and do *that*
for yourself

in their name
in *their* honor
love yourself
as they loved you

they would like that

on those days
when you miss someone the most
love yourself harder.

KEEP IT SIMPLE

Keep it simple
your life
you can only do so much
and the simple things are there to fuel your heart
when the waves of overwhelm
start to crash against your wall
keep it simple
you can only do so much

it's the simple, everyday
that will help you on your way
look around
take in the moment
be at ease
when the winds of worry roar
against the castle you have built
take a rest
feel your heartbeat
be at peace

keep it simple
your life
you can only do so much
and the little things are there to bring you joy
when the hounds of dark and dread
begin to howl inside your mind
keep it simple
you can only do so much.

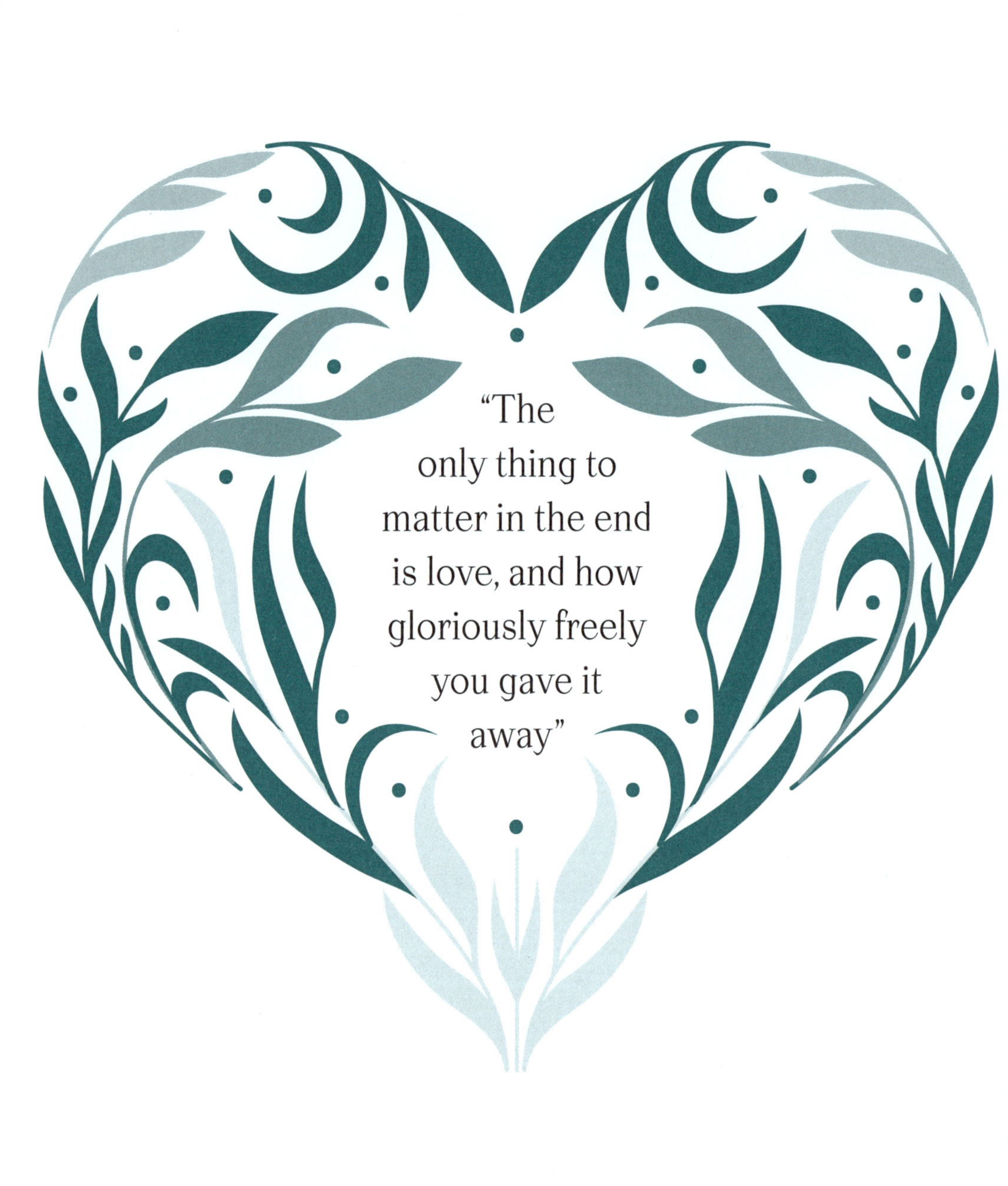
"The only thing to matter in the end is love, and how gloriously freely you gave it away"

EARLY

Those who face their final days on this earth will look you deep in the eyes and tell you none of it matters. That the only thing to matter in the end is love, and how gloriously freely you gave it away, to yourself too. They will grab your hands and try to squeeze this all-encompassing, earth-shattering truth into your very bones. Let them. They are close enough to the veil to see the answer, the reason, the why, and their only wish in that precious, fleeting moment is that they could enlighten you early. Let them, my loves, let them.

I feel like

the sun

is

shining

on me when

you're near

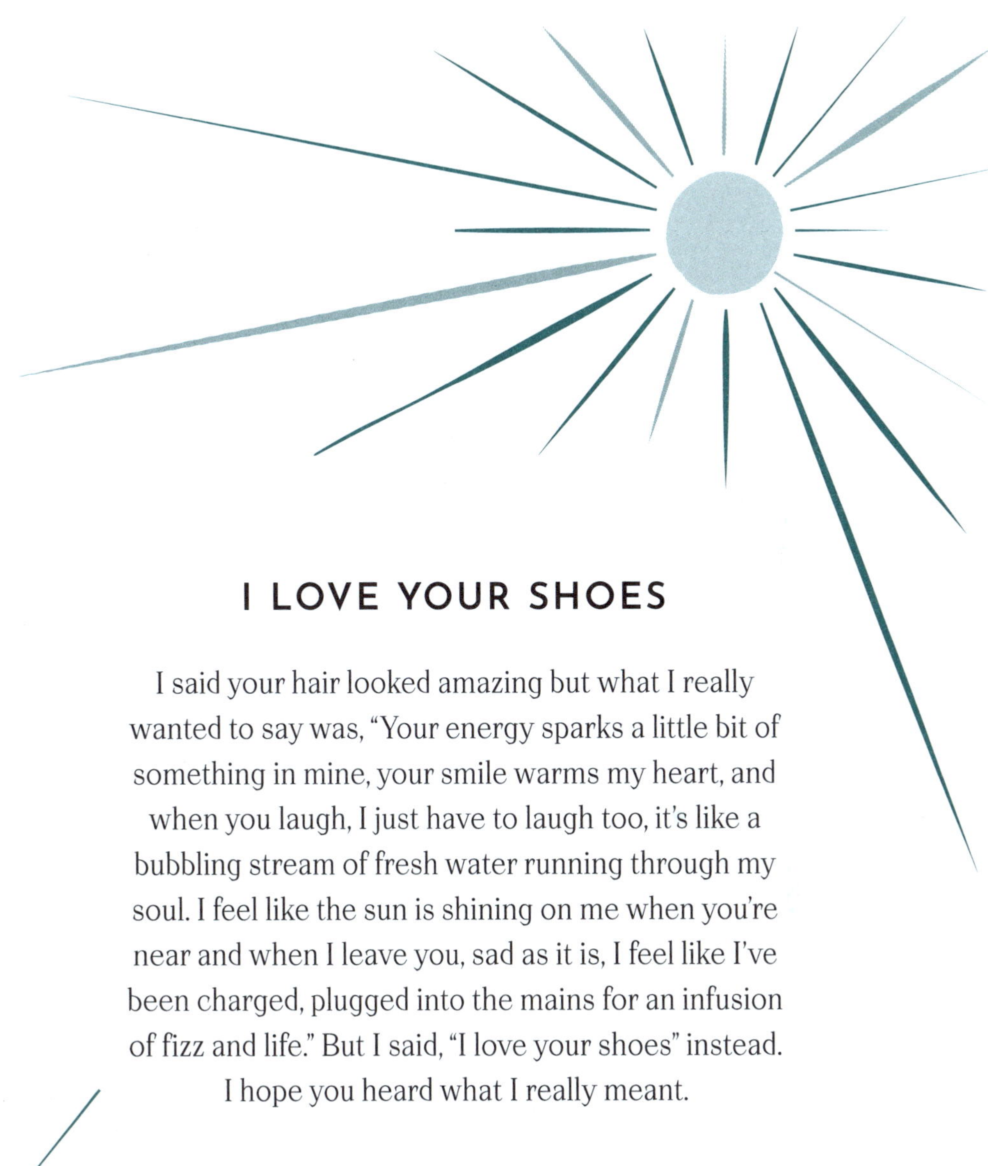

I LOVE YOUR SHOES

I said your hair looked amazing but what I really wanted to say was, "Your energy sparks a little bit of something in mine, your smile warms my heart, and when you laugh, I just have to laugh too, it's like a bubbling stream of fresh water running through my soul. I feel like the sun is shining on me when you're near and when I leave you, sad as it is, I feel like I've been charged, plugged into the mains for an infusion of fizz and life." But I said, "I love your shoes" instead. I hope you heard what I really meant.

SELF-WORTH

Don't hitch your self-worth to something that moves, a number, a dress size, a person, a talent. Your self-worth is the most valuable thing you own and should be secured, fastened tight, to something solid. Something unshakeable. Grow that self-worth well, my love, and weld it with power to the very inside of your being, your soul, your essence. Give it space to grow bigger still but let no one have access, other than you. You don't share your self-worth with anyone, ever. If they want to grow their own, you can help them just by leading, by showing the way, by living the example they seek. Don't hitch your self-worth to something that moves. It's the biggest asset you own.

LISTEN FOR THE LOVE

We don't always say *I love you*
sometimes we say
you're not eating very well
or *should you be going out in this weather?*

we don't always say
you're amazing
sometimes we say
I wish you would believe in yourself more

we don't always say *I love you*
sometimes, we open our mouths
and our hearts
(which are actually full of love)
pour out critically
nagging, berating, moaning, smothering

we can work on that

sometimes, love doesn't always sound like
I love you
sometimes it sounds like
eat more vegetables
be home by nine
don't work so hard

listen for the love in everything you hear today
it doesn't always sound like it should
but it's there
it's there.

"They are with
you, and they
burn brightly
with their
boundless light
in everything
you do"

THE WOMEN BEFORE

It is not just your mother who may walk with you in spirit, it is her mother too, and her mother's mother. And her mother's friends, who loved by choice and not blood. And the women before them. Generations and generations of female energy, watching in admiration as you forge ahead, living *better*, feeling *better*, accepting *better* than they ever did. As they very much hoped you would. So, when you feel low, lonely or unloved, remember them, *feel* them. They are with you, and they burn brightly with their boundless light, in everything you do. You, my friends, are the "moment in time" of many women gone before, and you will lay pathways, like they did, for those who come up next. What a beautiful, unending legacy.

"Whatever
comes our
way, is not
enough, to
separate
this love"

I CHOOSE YOU

I choose you, every day. That's really all there is to say. It's simple. Whatever comes our way, is not enough, to separate this love. And anything that rocks us, won't be more, than the blood and bones we used to forge our core. I choose you, every day and always will. I'll let this love we made rise up and spill, into the life we share together, making shelter for harsh weather. And as we stand here hearts in hands, let's agree: to grow stronger every moment we are we. Like penguins are forever, we will be. Forever choosing you, and forever hoping you'll choose me.

BE THE PEACE

When the world outside is in disarray and chaos abounds, it is vital that you live the life you dream of in your own little bubble. Make the world you want. Kindness, love, patience, acceptance and care. Throw it around like confetti and create the world you will not see on the news. You cannot fix the world or change everyone's mind but you can be the peace you seek. And it is beyond vital that you do. It spreads like ever increasing ripples outwards and will find those like-hearted souls you need to reach. When the world is in unrest, be the peace you seek.

SURPRISE

Things people love about you
may come as a surprise…

it's not the accolades you achieve
the number of friends you have
or how many invitations come your way
it's not that you are well behaved or uncomplicated
or even that you work hard

it's your laugh,
the way you make that funny sound
when something has really tickled you just right
it's the face you make when you're thinking
the singing you do when you think no one is listening
and that mirror pout you pull without realizing

it's the way you get passionate about *your* stuff
the determination you have against adversity

it's the kindness you show to someone in need
the way you can never pass an animal without getting soppy

it's the fact that you have irrational fears and beliefs
that make no sense whatsoever
but they are *yours*, so they matter

the things that people love about you
may come as a surprise

they are all the things you don't even have to strive for.

It’s the face you make when you’re thinking

"You need
fresh, open
spaces with
room to
breathe"

CAGE

Sometimes things crumble around you not because you are losing everything, but because the life you built has become your cage. And you don't need a cage, my friend, you don't need a cage. You need fresh, open spaces with room to breathe, room to roam, room to reach out and room to grow. Sometimes things crumble around you simply because you built them too well. Let it crumble. It no longer serves you and it's high time you broke out.

"The joy
of living
you see
is free"

JOIE DE VIVRE

Like scientists with the atom
and mathematicians with pi
we have long studied
this enigmatic essence of joy

we tick lists and boxes
dot the i's and strike the t's
mind our q's and our p's

and wait patiently for its coming

we create tantalizing tableaus
and lust-worthy lives
and if everything is perfect
we pray joy will materialize

tempted by our sacrificial offerings

but we forget
in the rush around this doing
that joy favors those blatantly being

that the only act this gift requires
is your precious holy breathing

the joy of living, you see
is free
the point, the why
the *joie de vivre.*

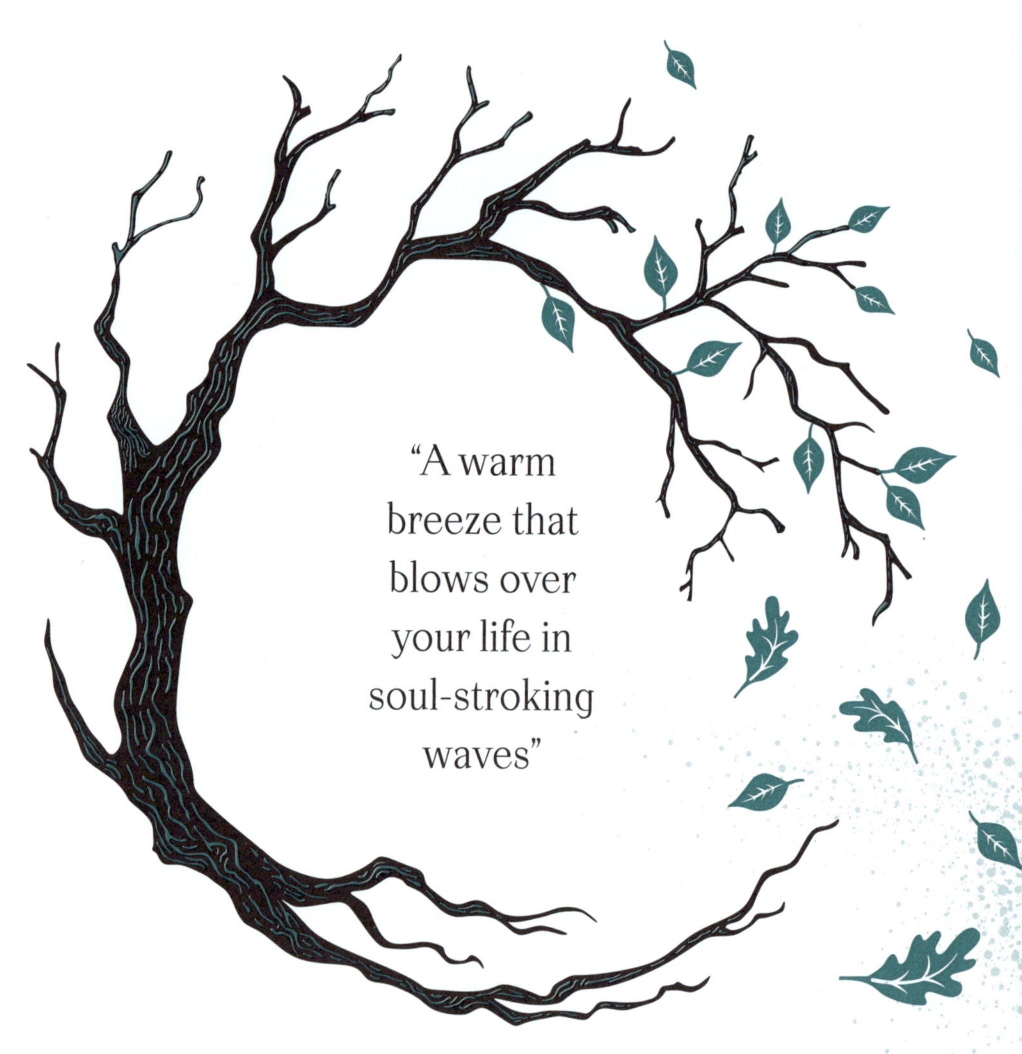

"A warm
breeze that
blows over
your life in
soul-stroking
waves"

WARM BREEZE

Happiness is not a constant state of being. It's a warm breeze that blows over your life in soul-stroking waves, in between all the other emotions. Happiness is a weather front, not a place. And it should come and go. Because your garden, whether you realize it or not, needs all the weathers to stay healthy. You don't become *happy*, my friends. You become content, peaceful, accepting. Which simply means, when that warm breeze of happiness blows your way, you're ready to tilt your face up - and feel it.

"The bravest
thing you can
do is be kind
to yourself
when you
feel you
deserve it
the *least*"

HOW YOU GROW

The bravest thing you can do
is be kind to yourself
when you feel
you deserve it
the *least*

when you are imperfect
when you have failed

when you are off track
out of whack
and flawed

if you can find
that grain of kindness
for your most unloveable self
it will land
like blessed raindrops
on a parched plant

and that, my friend
is how you grow.

"You're
trailing
a bright
pathway
that you
don't even
know about"

YOU

If every single person who has liked you in your lifetime were to light up on a map, it would create the most glitteringly beautiful network you could imagine. Throw in the strangers you've been kind to, the people you've made laugh or inspired along the way, and that star-bright web of **you** would be an impressive sight to behold. You're so much more than you think you are. You have done so much more than you realize. You're trailing a bright pathway that you don't even know about. What a thing. *What a thing indeed.*

CHANGE

My friend
when change threatens
to whip the rug
from under your feet
or push you out
of your comfortable bubble
face it

look change
right in the eye
and let it know
that you have been changing
every day
since the day you were born
and you will do so
until the day you die

and you may not be quite ready
for this particular change *yet*
but you're not afraid

because you have done this many times

change got you where you are now

and look how far you've come.

"Love wins
if we let it
if we never
forget it"

LOVE WINS

What if we just vow that love will win? From the moment we begin to fall. What if we decide to overlook all the small and go straight to the core? Pledging to pick one another up off of the floor. And to never ignore. What if we agree to be we, without shaving off the edges of you, the edges of me? And always respecting our souls must be free. What if ... we see love as the ocean and we are the ship? Can we adventure and plan? Sometimes gracing the land, to restore? Then back sailing again to the more. Love wins, if we let it, if we never forget it. Let's never forget it, okay? When our branches are swayed. Let our roots be well laid.

ALIVE

We each of us know we are going to die
yet we daily wake up
wondering why
we are here
as though the mission we have
is not strikingly clear
we are simply born to live
and as we live
to see how much love we can give
and receive
to see if we can still believe
despite daily distractions
and subtractions
to our soul
can we believe we are always whole?
and that just being is the goal?
we each of us know we are going to die
so let's get on
with the very serious matter
of feeling alive.

AFTERWORD

Thank you for breathing life into these pages. A book's heart begins to beat when it is written, but the reader is the air within its lungs. It's an honor to share this wild, twisting ride with you. Whenever life feels heavy or hard, crack this book open - I'll be here, walking beside you. And on the days when the sun graces your face, crack her open then too, to honor the joy. It is truly vital that you do.

ACKNOWLEDGMENTS

It is hard to list my thanks when I am brimming over with them daily. Where do I begin?

To all my loves, for whom my soul gives gratitude every day. To my dear friends and wonderful family.

To the amazing people I am so lucky to meet on this journey. Each and every follower who comes to my events imparts such energy into my soul that I am never left empty or exhausted. I listen to everything you so openly share with me and it is channeled back into the words we all need and use. It is an exchange, this thing, not just me speaking to you. Never just me speaking to you. Gratitude is infused into every word I write. I hope you feel it.

Special thanks to my Susanna and publishing team at Bonnier Books, who have supported and cared for me for the past few years. Friendships took root immediately, of course, as is the way of these things. And the magic of that blooming undoubtedly came through the pages of the books we set to print. Forever glad we met and created what we did. A big thank-you too to Studio Nic&Lou for the beautifully designed pages and cover of this book.

To my husband, Robert, who has taken my new-found busyness in his stride and helped so much with the day-to-day tasks so I may adventure wherever this ride takes me. You are the safety net; you always catch me when I fall. And I always fall.

To my sister, Nanette, who is never far from my side and whom many of you have had the pleasure of meeting. You are the ocean to my fire, and I am so very lucky to have had your flow to follow for all these years.

Am I allowed to thank my pets? They truly bring me joy and affection in every moment and consistently remind me what the point is: love. If you are cradling a broken heart, they have the glue. If I could give one piece of advice to anyone seeking more happiness, it would be to love an animal. They are it.

To the incredible people I have met along this way and to my beloved Davina McCall for always championing me and allowing me to blaze her support across my covers. You have been such a bright light on this path, and I have danced in its beam every day.

I'd also love to acknowledge Jennae Cecilia for her viral prompt, "I Met My Younger Self for a Coffee." I was inspired to write my own, along with thousands of other women. I think it did us all good.

It is hard to list thanks when you wake up every day absolutely fit to bursting with them. Just please know, I am grateful. And I will show it in the way I know best: words.

And on that note, I close this book, but please do take another look, at random, when the storms roll in… there's magic, love and joy within.

LIST OF POEMS BY COLLECTION

WILD HOPE

Happy
Magic
Joy Chose You
Before You Sleep
You Are Nature
The Edge
Spring
Summer
Autumn
Wintering
Good
In Rest, They Remember
Too Many Sundays
Forgotten Gravy
A Day Is Not Lost
In the Photo
Wildlings
Awakening
Right Now
Just a Day
The Witch Wound
A Handful of Years
The After-Party People
Love Came First
The Women Before
You

GROWING BRAVE

Yellow
You'll Be Okay
Angels
Joy Comes Back
The Taker of the Photo
Zoom In
You Just Grew
Friend Ship
Sadness Comes
She Sent
This Platonic Song
Forever Days
I Want to Listen
Bruise
Warm Breeze

JOY CHOSE YOU

Now
Sitting with Joy
Confetti
Speak Less
Already Here
Eclipse of Grief
None of Your Business
This Little Moment
A Little Weird
Small Joys
Roots of Sisterhood
Feathers That Flew
Bedfellows
Coffee with My Younger Self
Other Girls
Serendipity
Soul Tribe
Early
I Choose You
Be the Peace
Joie de Vivre
Love Wins
Alive

ABOUT THE AUTHOR

Donna Ashworth is a *Sunday Times* best-selling poet who lives in the hills of Scotland with her husband, two sons, Brian and Dave (the dogs) and Sheldon and Mani (the cats). Donna started her social media accounts in 2018 in a bid to create a "safe" social space for women to come together and connect, but her love of all things wordy quickly became the focus, and a past love for poetry was reignited. More than 10 books and nearly 2 million followers later, Donna is delighted daily with her mission to shower the world with words and make poetry a go-to in our well-being tool kit.

"I believe wholeheartedly in the power of opening a daily poetry page to better everyone's mental health and clear space within our minds. Poetry is permission to feel everything we as humans are absolutely supposed to, knowing we are not alone, never alone. Poetry is not folly for the fancy; it is using words to shift perspectives, heal wounds and let in light again. And it is something we can pass to one another when times become turbulent, as they so often will. Open this book at random, whenever you need a message or a focus or a sign… the book just knows. As do you, my friends, as do you."

Facebook @DonnaAshworth
Instagram @DonnaAshworthWords
TikTok @DonnaAshworthWordy
X @donna_ashworth

I'll be

here

walking

beside

you

We hope you enjoyed this Hay House book. If you'd like to receive our online catalog featuring additional information on Hay House books and products, or if you'd like to find out more about the Hay Foundation, please contact:

Hay House LLC, P.O. Box 5100, Carlsbad, CA 92018-5100
(760) 431-7695 or (800) 654-5126
www.hayhouse.com® • www.hayfoundation.org

Published in Australia by:
Hay House Australia Publishing Pty Ltd
18/36 Ralph St., Alexandria NSW 2015
Phone: +61 (02) 9669 4299
www.hayhouse.com.au

Published in the United Kingdom by:
Hay House UK Ltd
1st Floor, Crawford Corner,
91–93 Baker Street, London W1U 6QQ
Phone: +44 (0)20 3927 7290
www.hayhouse.co.uk

Published in India by:
Hay House Publishers (India) Pvt Ltd
Muskaan Complex, Plot No. 3,
B-2, Vasant Kunj, New Delhi 110 070
Phone: +91 11 41761620
www.hayhouse.co.in